PRAISE FOR *THINK OR SINK:*

"Thinking is the highest function you are capable of. This book will help you improve every aspect of your life. Buy two and give one to a friend."

– Bob Proctor, from the movie *The Secret* and Author of *Born Rich*

"The concepts are presented clearly and the focus on the importance of leaning to self-regulate emotions is right on target. Learning to manage our thoughts and emotions from a new more intelligent inner reference point represents the next step in unlocking improved human health and performance."

– Dr. Rollin McCraty, Director of Research, HeartMath Research Center

"Gina's book teaches us how to perceive crisis as opportunity and hardship as the bridge to healing. She does the math for us, so that all we have to do is show up ready for this mind-shifting, spiritual education!"

– Meredith Scott Lynn, Actress/Producer/Director

"A combination of intellectual, international entrepreneur, wife and mother, Gina represents the new model for women: someone who does it all. Remarkable!"

– Mary Aitken, CEO and Founder of Verity

Think *or* Sink

~~~~~~~

THE ONE CHOICE THAT
CHANGES EVERYTHING

Think *or* Sink

THE ONE CHOICE THAT CHANGES EVERYTHING

BY

GINA MOLLICONE-LONG

STERLING & ROSS PUBLISHERS

NEW YORK

Published by
Sterling & Ross Publishers
New York, NY 10001
www.sterlingandross.com

Paperback original.

This publication is designed to educate and provide general information regarding the subject matter covered. It is not intended to replace the counsel of other professional advisors. The reader is encouraged to consult with his or her own advisors regarding specific situations. While the author has taken reasonable precautions in the preparation of this book and believes the facts presented within the book are accurate, neither the publisher nor author assumes any responsibility for errors or omissions. The author and publisher specifically disclaim any liability resulting from the use or application of the information contained in this book. The information within this book is not intended to serve as emotional or therapeutic advice related to individual situations.

For bulk or special sales, please contact: sales@sterlingandross.com

Library of Congress Cataloging-in-Publication Data

Mollicone-Long, Gina, 1970-
Think or sink / by Gina Mollicone-Long.
p. cm.
ISBN 978-0-9821392-1-9 (pbk.)
1. Choice (Psychology) 2. Decision making. 3. Opportunity. I. Title.
BF611.M646 2010
153.8'3--dc22
2009036697

Cover design: The Book Designers
Book editor & design: Rachel Trusheim
HeartMath graphic used with permission
Interior illustration: Aritz Bermudez Monfort

10 9 8 7 6 5 4 3 2

Printed in the United States of America

This book is dedicated to my children, Molly and Simon.

May you always meet life's greatest challenges with an even greater strength from within yourselves.

ACKNOWLEDGMENTS

"If I have seen further than others, it is
because I have stood on the shoulders of giants."
– Sir Isaac Newton

This book would not have happened without the support and encouragement of many, many people. I am deeply grateful to the following people. First, to my husband, Andrew, and my children, Molly and Simon. Thank you for providing me the space to do my work in such a loving and supportive way. To my parents and siblings for always believing in me even when you don't understand me. To all of my in-laws (mother, father, brother, sister) for supporting me as one of your own. To Drew, Rachel and the rest of the crew at Sterling & Ross, your enthusiasm for this project is awesome. To Dr. Rollin McCraty at the Institute of HeartMath for your generous insight, wisdom, intelligence and ground-breaking research. To Betty, Xiaolan and Janice for supporting me to be the best version of myself possible. To the staff and fellow members at Verity for providing the sanctuary for most of this writing. To Jennifer Smith for helping me to see the possibility of doing this project with a publisher. To Alana Diebel for making such an imprint on my life and for reading the very first draft. To Danielle Hampton and Janet Doucette for your insights. To Stacey, Amy, Erin and all of our staff at Critical Pathfinders and Goddess Concepts. To Kirk and Lou for making the very serendipitous introduction to Drew many years ago. To Bob Hamilton from Drumheller for helping me to clarify the synopsis on that WestJet flight. To Roxolana for inspiring the first book that was the foundation for this one. To Bob Proctor for your abundant support. To my girl power author team of Denise, Carolyn and Sonia for being there for me. To Jane Roos, Vicki Saunders and Bruce Sellery for unquestioningly supporting me whenever I ask. To Dr. Mihaly Csikszentmihaly for helping to clarify my research. To Drs. Tad and Adriana James for holding me to the highest standard of excellence. To Sara Genn for being my soul sister. For Kathy Kortes-Miller for showing me the true meaning of strength. To Seton Montgomerie for being present when things were redefining themselves. To Ryan Strom for keeping up with all of my electronic requests. To all of my clients and participants for allowing me the honor to share in your lives and to glimpse your greatness. And again, to my husband Andrew, especially for the hours and hours of editing and life-saving hugging. I would be nowhere without you.

CONTENTS

CHAPTER ONE

~~~~~~~

THIS IS WHAT OPPORTUNITY
FEELS LIKE

"The world is round, and the place which may seem
like the end may also be the beginning."

– Ivy Baker Priest

The paradox of any challenge or crisis is that it is also an opportunity. This might seem crazy at first, but I will show you in the next nine chapters how to turn your adversity into your advantage. A crisis can be any situation of extreme difficulty or danger like losing a job, suffering a divorce or falling ill. During challenging times many people look for and focus on what is wrong. Not only is this perspective harmful because it doesn't bring about any solutions or relief, but it is also the very thing that ensures the continuation of the crisis itself. That's right, focusing on what's wrong will always bring about more of what's wrong. Conversely then, (and great news) is that focusing on what's right will also bring about more of what's right. This is the opportunity that lies within crisis: if you learn to observe it, interpret it and leverage the lessons inherent in it, then crisis can be integral to achieving success and inner happiness.

It all comes down to choice—your choice of how you will

respond. The most important thing that you can do during a challenging time is to become the master of your mind and emotions. You must learn to react outside of your automatic default responses to crisis and to engage all of your creative faculties, problem-solving skills and coping abilities. Failure to think while you are facing any crisis or challenge will only serve to exacerbate the very circumstances that you are trying to change. You will sink into a looping cycle of crisis and reaction that never leads to resolution. The only way out of the crisis or challenge is right through the middle of it. Your problem will cease to be a problem when you discover within yourself the resources that you need to handle it.

There are three states that I consider to be the birthright of every human being. They are *peace, love and joy,* and they are the core of who you are. We often perceive any challenge, crisis or failure as a threat to our right to experience these states. However, challenges, crises and failures do not have to inhibit our ability to achieve peace, love and joy. Instead, such negative circumstances can serve us in their ability to demonstrate to us, sometimes very emphatically, that we may be lacking a vital connection to our natural states in our lives. Instead of wishing that your circumstances were different, use them as a cue that you are being challenged to find new resources within yourself.

> "Failure is just another way to learn how to do something right."
> – Marian Wright Edelman

I want to reiterate what I just said because for many it represents a significant paradigm shift. And one you <u>must</u> make if you are to find any power in a crisis. *A crisis, failure or challenge* can <u>*always*</u> *serve you because it highlights, in plain view, what is* <u>*missing.*</u> Once you know what is missing then you can take the necessary steps to get it.

Now, please don't misunderstand me. I didn't say that crises and challenges feel good. In fact, they always feel awful, sometimes even devastating. Not something you'd choose off a menu of experiences. However, they are gifts. Always! They are gifts because they give you an opportunity to make a major shift in your life. Now, some of you might be saying, "What if I don't want to make a shift? I like things the way they are." I can respect that. The issue is this: you can't remain in one place forever because as a human being you are always moving. You are either moving forward or moving backward, but you are always moving. You may have heard the saying, "You're either growing or you're dying." You are allowed to choose between them, but just be clear that you are choosing. If you're like most of us, you would choose to grow rather than die. Let's take a moment here to define what growth really means. In this context, it means finding new resources within yourself that enable you to cope with stressful circumstances easily and effortlessly. You should understand then that crisis and challenge in your life are part of the growth process. They serve the purpose of facilitating your growth.

> "Just when the caterpillar thought the world was over, it became a butterfly."
>
> – Author unknown

GROWTH TRIGGERS

When things go wrong, you are usually forced to develop a new way of Being. This process ultimately leads to the discovery of resources that were unknown up to this point. I am often quoted and interviewed on the topic of self-esteem, especially with respect to schools. My viewpoint is that self-esteem doesn't come from a failure-less environment. Rather self-esteem comes in the moment when you fall flat on your face and you decide to get back up. In that moment, you find out that you are made of more than you thought you were. This new knowledge is what raises your self-esteem. Falling down was the trigger that forced you to find new resources, a new way of Being or a new perspective.

There is a type of plant that grows in Australia known as the Banksia. An interesting quality of most species of Banksia is that the seed pods can only be opened by the heat of a bush fire. Many people would share the viewpoint that a bush fire is an undesirable event. However, the Banksia can only release its seeds after a devastating fire. The bush fire acts as a trigger for the Banksia to release its seeds and grow. No fire—no seeds—no growth. In the case of the Banksia, the fire is a good thing. Without the fire, the Banksia never finds out what it can really do. Get it?

When things fall apart, then something isn't working. It indicates that the structure wasn't sustainable, so it broke. For example, let's say a child is building a tower made of wooden blocks. She starts with one block on the bottom and then puts two blocks on top of the one, then three on top of two, then four on top of three. You can see where this is going. Eventually, her tower will fall over because it isn't sustainable. The crashing of her tower is feedback that she needs to try a different approach. Sooner or later, she will discover that it makes much more sense to build a tower of blocks on a solid foundation.

The toppling of her tower wasn't her real problem. Her <u>real</u> problem was that she tried to build an unstable tower. The experience allowed her to grow, expand her knowledge and search for a way to <u>build a better tower</u>.

CRISIS IS OPPORTUNITY

This book is not full of blithe advice about how mere positive thinking in times of trouble is your salvation. Nor is this book meant to belittle your suffering in any way. This book is about a paradigm shift. When you shift into the perspective that crisis and challenge are there to serve your growth, then you can be more powerful when experiencing difficult circumstances. You can make sense of your suffering and you can actually take steps to come out of it.

You can love the life you live once you learn how to access peace, love or joy regardless of what is going on in your reality. We need to learn how to override some of our programs and reverse some outdated and incorrect paradigms so that we can have access to peace, love or joy whenever we choose. I do not use the term "choose" loosely because it is my ardent belief that we have the power to choose our way of Being at any given moment. This book is your step-by-step guide to turning those times of seeming powerlessness and disappointment into sources of strength, happiness and growth.

Every single human being has a hardwired response to challenge, crisis and failure. Where many people run into difficulty is that at some point during their lives, they have developed inappropriate responses to certain situations. In a sense, the problem is <u>over</u>reacting (or even underreacting).

People who are able to come to their senses during a crisis and think clearly will be able to find a solution and peace of mind more easily than those who remain stuck. Therefore, if you want to find a solution to your problem, you need to become a master at regulating your reaction in any given situation. This is the only way to become aware and access new resources. You must learn to think for yourself and recognize when your response is appropriate and when your response is excessive. If you are not conscious of your response, then you can sink into your default response to the situation or the general consensus of the people around you.

RESPONSES DEFINED

We are always responding to external events, whether we are aware of it or not. Our mind is constantly processing external information and matching it up against the models that we have created to determine if there is a match. A match to the model is a signal that we are comfortable and no adjustment is required. The issue arises when there is a mismatch to the model. Any external event that does not match the model creates a stressful situation as the mind attempts to sort, identify and classify the incoming stimuli so that we can return to our comfort zone. For example, if you are used to driving to work without traffic, then a traffic jam will signal a mismatch to your model and this will launch a stress response.

There are two interesting facts to point out about this process. Firstly, that it is a <u>mismatch</u> to the model that causes the stress. It doesn't matter if the model itself is flawed; the mismatch is the important part. If the comfortable and familiar operating model for an individual is anxiety and uncertainty, then even an event as innocuous as quiet and calm could cause a mismatch and create stress for the individual. In that sense, the individual's model is a key factor in determining what will cause a mismatch and be classified as a stressful situation. The individual is unconsciously driven to experience anxiety states in order to feel comfortable.

The second important fact to note about response has to do with how the matching and mismatching gets determined. Until very recently, it was thought that only the conscious mind could process external stimuli and determine a match or mismatch. However, recent research at the Institute of HeartMath shows that we also process incoming stimuli on an emotional level and can determine a match or mismatch in a situation.[1] What is even more interesting is that this mechanism works at a much faster rate than the conscious mind, so a response to a situation can be initiated before we are really aware of the entire situation.

Consider then that what we call "stress" isn't a "thing" at all. In fact, no one has ever seen "stress." You can't put it into a wheelbarrow. So what is it? Stress actually is a response or a decision by you to classify something as "stressful." It doesn't have to be a conscious choice, but it is a choice nonethless.

HARDWIRED RESPONSES

The biological response of animals to threat is called "fight

---

1   McCraty, R. *Heart Brain Neurodynamics*. Institute of HeartMath, 2003.

or flight." The fight-or-flight response was first described in 1915 by Walter Cannon who was a professor and chairman of the Department of Physiology at Harvard Medical School. His theory showed that all animals, including human beings, respond to acute stress in the same manner: by preparing the body to run or to fight off the attack. This fight-or-flight response is hardwired into your physiology because it is an essential element in survival.

Because it is hardwired, it is typically unconscious, meaning that you don't really have to DO anything in order to activate your fight-or-flight response. You don't need to think about the threat consciously and then determine whether you should react with fight-or-flight. The reaction is preprogrammed into your physiology as a protective measure. This is good news and bad news. It's good news if you happen to suffer a serious acute attack because it will likely save your life. However, it is bad news when the response is activated inappropriately, like when the perceived threat is not a significant threat to your survival because the stress response depletes many of the body's resources.

The fight-or-flight response is a "stress response." The crisis produces stress and the body responds with fight-or-flight. The problem most of us have is that many situations produce a stress response even though the situations are usually not life-threatening. We are seeing an increase in the number of events that are labeled as "crises" or "stressful" in modern times compared with generations past. For example, CBS News reported that worker's compensation claims for "mental stress" in California rose 200–700 percent in the 1980s. As soon as an event is classified as "stress" then the body launches its hardwired response.

New research shows that we are also hardwired to react with empathy and compassion. The field of social neuroscience is showing us that this hardwired response of empathy gets blocked when our attention is focused on ourselves or our problems (i.e., a crisis or challenge). There was an intriguing study done many years ago at Princeton Theological Seminary showing this dynamic.[2] A group of divinity students were told they were going to give a practice sermon and they were each given a sermon topic. Half of the students were given the topic of the Good Samaritan—the biblical story about the man who stopped to help the stranger in need by the side of the road. The other half were given random bible topics. One by one, they were told when it was time to go and give their sermon. Some were told to rush and others were not. As they went from one building to the second building, each one passed a man who was bent over and moaning in need of assistance. It was found that over 60 percent of the seminarians passed by without stopping to help. It didn't matter at all whether or not they were contemplating the parable of the Good Samaritan. What actually determined whether someone would stop and help was how much of a hurry they thought they were in. Only 10 percent of those who were told to rush offered help, whereas 63 percent of those who thought they had extra time offered to help the man. This illustrates a new idea that is emerging that says our default empathetic response is affected by our focus; meaning that empathy and compassion gets trumped by a stress response.

---

2   Darley, John M. and C. Daniel Batson. "From Jerusalem to Jericho: A Study of Situational and Dispositional Variables in Helping Behaviour." 1970.

Our reaction to a stressful or compassionate event is actually a biological response. So, to understand how it works, it is best to start with a short lesson about our bodies. Please remember that I am outlining some basic functions of the body in very general terms in order to keep it simple. The full range of complexity of the human body is outside the scope of this material. Think of the next section as Basic Physiology.

THE AUTONOMIC NERVOUS SYSTEM (ANS)

Your autonomic nervous system (ANS) is a major control system in your body. The ANS affects things such as heart rate, digestion and respiration among other things. Most of the actions of the ANS are involuntary and do not require conscious thought at the basic level. This is very beneficial when it comes to regulating the body. Imagine if you had to remember to breathe every moment of every day. You wouldn't last very long when your mind became interested in another thought and wandered away from remembering to breathe. Your ANS is hardwired to take care of your biological functions to ensure your survival.

The ANS can be divided into two components: the sympathetic nervous system and the parasympathetic nervous system. Neither system is better than the other as both systems are very important and have distinct functions in the body. The sympathetic nervous system is the system that is activated when you are in fight-or-flight response. The sympathetic nervous system runs the show when you are in a crisis. The primary function of this response is to ensure your survival. To that end, sympathetic response includes shutting down or inhibiting all systems deemed "nonessential" to your survival. This list includes digestion, elimination and procreation, to name a few. One of the most interesting physical reactions to a threat is the loss of peripheral vision, meaning that when you are in fight-or-flight mode you have "tunnel vision" and your senses are heightened. This is so you can be attuned to any further danger. You essentially lose your access to creativity in this state because your body has focused all of its energy to ensure you can run away or stay and fight.

On the other hand, the parasympathetic system has been nicknamed the "rest-and-digest" system. The parasympathetic system is responsible for regulating digestion, elimination and normal functioning and behavior. People often view these two systems as being in opposition to each other. It is more accurate to think of them as complementary systems. The sympathetic system is mainly concerned with functions requiring quick response, whereas the parasympathetic system is concerned with functions that do not require immediate response. The best analogy is that of a sprinter (sympathetic) versus a long-distance runner (parasympathetic).

HYPOTHALMUS-PITUITARY-ADRENAL AXIS

The hypothalamus-pituitary-adrenal (HPA) axis is a complex set of interactions between three organs: the hypothalamus, the pituitary gland and the adrenal glands. Your hypothalamus is located just above your brain stem and is responsible for connecting your nervous system to your endocrine (hormonal) system. Your pituitary gland is an endocrine gland about the size of a pea located near the bottom of the hypothalamus in your brain.

The pituitary gland is sometimes called the "master" gland of the endocrine system, because it controls the functions of the other endocrine glands. Finally, your adrenal glands are star-shaped endocrine glands that sit on top of your kidneys. They are mainly responsible for regulating the stress response through the production of hormones, including cortisol, adrenaline and DHEA (dehydroepiandrosterone).

The HPA axis is the hormonal pathway the brain and adrenal glands use to communicate with each other. It is one of the two main pathways involved in the stress response.

THE PHYSIOLOGY OF STRESS

The first thing that happens when you perceive a threat is that your adrenal glands release adrenaline which results in an increase in your breathing rate, your heart rate and your blood pressure. This serves to move more blood to the muscles needed for fighting or running. Your senses also become more acute in order to detect further

> *"Tension is who you think you should be. Relaxation is who you are."*
>
> *– Chinese proverb*

danger. This is the fight-or-flight response to the stressor event and was quite adequate for most of our evolution when the stressors or threats were short-lived as in the case of a saber-toothed tiger attack. The idea of "chronic stress" is a modern issue in that we can't easily escape our stressors because they are recurring (i.e., debt). In addition, we perceive many more instances as threats. All of this leads to an overworked fight-or-flight or stress response.

Adrenaline can cause problems as it prepares you for action by diverting resources to the muscles from the areas of the body that carry out long-term body maintenance. As with any machine, regular maintenance is key to optimal performance. If you are constantly diverting your maintenance resources for a crisis, then it will eventually take its toll on your health. Increased adrenaline also interferes with clear judgment and makes it difficult to take the time to make good decisions. It also causes difficult situations to be seen as a threat, not a challenge. When your adrenaline levels are increased, your senses become keener and you are dedicated to discovering any other sources of threat, but you lose the ability to see the "big picture." You need to be able to maintain big-picture perspective in order to be able to discover new resources and solutions.

Adrenaline is a quick response hormone that has a short life. It doesn't spend much time in your system. However, if the stress is severe or persists for more than a few minutes, then your adrenal glands release cortisol. Cortisol has a much slower momentum (longer life), so that once it is released, it takes a very long time to clear from your system. Studies have shown that one release of cortisol into your system depresses your immune system for eight hours. Furthermore, according to world-renowned brain researcher, Robert M. Sapolsky, sustained stress can damage the part of your brain that is central to learning and memory.[3] Too much cortisol can prevent the brain from making memories or accessing already existing memories. The problem with excess cortisol is that once inside the brain, it remains there much

---

3   Sapolsky, Robert M., et al. "Hippocampal Damage Associated with Prolonged Glucocorticoid Exposure in Primates," *The Journal of Neuroscience*, September 1990, Ye(g): 2897-2902.

longer than adrenaline and continues to do damage to your brain cells long after the stressful situation is over.

The point here isn't to suggest that we should never have adrenaline or cortisol in our systems. The issue arises when adrenaline and cortisol get released inappropriately in situations that might not warrant a full stress response. Adrenaline plays a positive role when it is used to generate activity not associated with a threat. Adrenaline is what powers your speed in a race and is behind many of the pursuits that we would consider exciting, arousing and energetic. Your body is fully capable of clearing itself of adrenaline and cortisol so that no damage ensues. The problem arises when you are constantly releasing these hormones into the system without sufficient periods of renewal.

DHEA

DHEA is another hormone produced by the adrenal glands and is the precursor to testosterone and estrogen. Precursors are hormones the body uses to produce other hormones.

In addition, DHEA has been linked to the immune system and well-being. Scientific research has shown that adequate levels of DHEA in the body can slow the aging process and prevent and/or improve some chronic health conditions. "DHEA is undeniably one of the most crucial predictive factors in diagnosing aging-related diseases," according to Ronald Klatz, D.O., president of the American Academy of Anti-Aging Medicine.

DHEA levels peak at the ages of 20–30 and then begin a natural decline. When our bodies produce cortisol and adrenaline during our stress response, DHEA production declines. DHEA protects your body from the hormone cortisol and the stress that triggers its production. DHEA and cortisol have an inverse relationship. When you're under continued stress, your cortisol/DHEA ratio goes up. This means that the excess cortisol is damaging DHEA's protective shield. The cortisol/DHEA ratio is used as a measure of health and aging. The lower this ratio, the better your overall health.

It seems that we should be trying to preserve and produce DHEA as much as possible. One way to maintain an optimal cortisol/DHEA ratio is to reduce the amount of adrenaline and, more importantly, cortisol that gets released into your system. This ultimately means reducing the number of situations that initiate your stress response. Given that you can only control your response to these circumstances, not the circumstances themselves, then becoming conscious of what you consider stressful and managing that stress without overtaxing your stress response is essential. The other way to boost this ratio is to increase DHEA production through positive empathetic and compassionate responses, which are impeded in the presence of a stress response.

RETICULAR ACTIVATING SYSTEM

Your reticular activating system (RAS) is the automatic mechanism inside your brain that brings relevant information to your attention. It is situated at the core of the brain stem between the medulla and midbrain. It is a little bundle of cells in the back of your brain that is known as the "control center" and it filters what enters your consciousness.

Your supply of attention is limited. You are literally being bombarded with an incredible amount of information every second of every day. In fact, Hungarian psychologist Mihalyi Csikszentmihalyi estimates that we can only consciously process about 126 bits of information per second.[4] This was based on earlier work by Miller (1956) and Orme (1969) and von Uexkull (1957). Miller showed that we could process seven (plus or minus two) chunks of information per unit of time. Then, Orme showed that an "attentional unit" of time was 1/18th of a second based on earlier calculations by von Uexkull. Therefore, we can process about 7 x 18 = 126 bits of information per second. It is estimated that there are millions of bits of information available to you in any given second. Yikes! You might be wondering what happens to the rest of the majority of information in every second of every day? It gets filtered out through a process of deletion, distortion and generalization in order for you to make sense of all the information. The RAS is the self-filtering system in charge of sorting the information and it chooses what you accept and reject based upon your beliefs, values and attitudes. The information that remains in your attention forms your "internal representation" or "map" of reality. Some people refer to this as your "awareness."

The focus of your RAS is determined by you and your perception of your circumstances. As you can imagine, when you are in a state of crisis and your adrenaline is running high, you will be automatically instructing your RAS to search out more of what's wrong as a protective mechanism. As soon as your RAS detects more of what's wrong, then that sets in motion another activation of your fight-or-flight response, which leads to more adrenaline

---

4   Csikszentmihalyi, Mihaly. *Flow: The Psychology of Optimal Experience.* Harper Perennial Modern Classics, 2008.

(and cortisol) and further instructions to your RAS to keep focusing on what is wrong. The end result is that you get trapped in a vicious cycle of looking for what's wrong, finding it and looking for more of what's wrong, finding it and so on and so on.

> "What we see depends mainly on what we look for."
>
> – Sir John Lubbock

This mechanism can also work to your benefit. By consciously instructing yourself to look for what is right, you are essentially programming your RAS to seek and find this information. As you begin to notice the things that are going right, you will begin to produce the behavior necessary to help you override the vicious cycle mentioned above. This is a critical step in turning adversity into advantage.

FLOWER POWER

Make a point to look for flowers for just one day. They can be real flowers, pictures of flowers, songs about flowers, etc. Just consciously look for flowers for an entire day. Make note of what you find. If you're like most people, then you will be surprised at how many flowers were right in front of you the whole time. Perhaps the solutions to your challenges are also right in front of you? What would happen if you looked for solutions for an entire day?

PHYSIOLOGY OF INNER PEACE

We have already discussed some biochemicals that are involved during your hardwired fight-or-flight response including adrenaline, cortisol and DHEA. Increased adrenaline and cortisol and decreased DHEA can have adverse affects on your long-term health. However, there are other biochemicals in your body that do wonders for your health. They include the biochemicals that get released when your body is operating in an optimal fashion and NOT having a stress response. Responses such as compassion and empathy are examples of such states.

The following biochemicals are associated with health and well-being. They are also associated with creativity, happiness and hopefulness. Likewise, they are the biochemicals that are depleted or absent when we are suffering from depression and feeling overwhelmed and "stressed out."

i. Endorphins
Endorphins are neurochemicals occurring naturally in the brain that have analgesic properties similar to morphine. In fact, research studies have shown that endorphins can be up to 10 times stronger than morphine. Endorphins are released during exercise and rhythmic breathing like the type associated with meditation or yoga. This is the chemical that gives rise to the term "runner's high."

ii. Serotonin and Dopamine
These chemicals are the "feel good" neurotransmitters. Serotonin is considered the feel good, inner peace, well-being neurotransmitter. Optimal serotonin levels are required for all positive affective states and all balanced emotional conditions. Dopamine is your excitatory neurotransmitter. When your dopamine levels are

balanced, you experience heightened states of alertness and awareness.

iii. Anandamide

This neurotransmitter is released during deep levels of meditation and when we are experiencing something that is new. The name is taken from the Sanskrit word *ananda*, which means "bliss." Simply put, this is our bliss chemical and it expands our blissful experiences.

PATTERNS, PREDICTABILITY AND BEHAVIOR

Your internal representation is what ultimately dictates your behavior in any given situation. Earlier, I referred to your internal representation as a map of reality. Everyone experiences the world in a different way. In fact, I would argue that no two people possess the exact same model of reality. This is due to the infinite number of combinations of values, beliefs, events and interpretations that can influence each person. Just as the map of the world is not the actual place but rather a representation of that place, your map of reality is just that: a map. It is not reality in absolute but rather your interpretation or representation of reality so that it makes sense to you.

Another way of looking at human beings is as strategy machines. We all have literally thousands and thousands of strategies that we use on a daily basis to move through our lives. You have a strategy for getting up, for getting ready, for driving your car and brushing your teeth. Everything you do in your life is the result of your own strategy. Some of your strategies are more effective than others, but suffice to say that everything you do is dictated by your strategy about how to do it. Another way to think about your strategies is to call them "patterns." Over the years, you have developed patterns of behavior (strategies) that deliver the outcomes or results that you desire. To that end, your results or outcomes are predictable to the extent that you are able to replicate your patterns.

The first time that you do something can be classified as a "learning experience" because you don't have a pattern for achieving the desired outcome. If your first attempt fails, then you usually search for another way to accomplish your goal. Once you find a pattern that delivers your intended result, then you begin to strengthen that pattern. Over time, this pattern becomes the dominant way to produce the intended result.

A great metaphor for this process is to think of a hill covered with snow. The first time you want to take your sled down this hill, you have literally no restrictions on which path you should take down the hill. So, you sit upon your sled and blast down the hill. Now, if you happen to encounter a tree root or a rock on this path, then you will choose a different path down the hill for the next run. Once you have established a "good run" down the hill, then you will continue to run your sled down the same path because it takes less effort than always choosing a new path. After time, your sled run will become a well-worn path and efficient way down the hill. This path will become a pattern and the outcome will be predictable: you will always end up in the same place at the end of your path. Think of each sled track down the hill as a neurological pattern; some are more worn than others, but all paths represent the same process. The outcome is predictable based on the patterns that precede them. It is not possible for you to take your sled down one path on the hill and end up at the end of another path. In the same way, all results in your life are unique to the behavior pattern that precedes them.

A SPECIAL NOTE ON FEAR

Interestingly, being afraid that something might happen is enough to evoke the same response as if it were actually happening. This is partly because the RAS cannot distinguish between events that are actually happening and events that are being imagined or visualized. It is also due to the way that we define and classify events as per our internal representation of reality. Fear can stop you from moving forward in your life because it evokes a fight-or-flight response, which dictates that you need to focus on survival instead of growth. Fear is created by our minds in an effort to keep us safe. It is a mechanism for preventing our demise when we sense danger. If we weren't afraid of the saber-toothed tiger, then we could just walk up and pat him on the back. We'd be his lunch pretty soon, so fear is a way of indicating that danger. When someone is in a state of fear, they are very easy to control due to the fact that they have limited resources available to them in the stress response that is created. Given that they lose the ability to think critically or see the "bigger picture" they default to any instruction being given to them since they are concerned only with their survival. Fear has been used in the past to control and direct people's thinking and behavior.

> *"Fear is an acronym for False Evidence Appearing Real."*
>
> *– Author unknown*

Again, it's not that we should erase our fears completely; chances are, we wouldn't last very long. Fear does have a protective function. However, it is the inappropriate fear response that is detrimental to our well-being. Just like a stress response, a fear response is appropriate in many situations. The issues arise when we begin to overreact to situations that don't warrant a fear response. Inappropriate fear stops you from doing things that might be beneficial and enjoyable for you. Fear can prevent you from living a life that you love.

The good news is that you can learn to be free of fear. You can learn to acknowledge your fear instead of having it control you. The key to being free of fear is to get out of our heads and back into our bodies in the present moment. When we are present to what is actually happening we are no longer controlled by our preestablished patterns. This presence gives us the ability to act *in spite of* our fear and to see options we might otherwise have missed. We can keep moving while being aware of our fear and using this awareness to inform our next move.

To say that I have a fear of heights is a gross understatement. Thousands of people who have been in my audiences have heard me describe in detail how I lose feeling in my legs when I get about 10 feet off the ground. I once did the CN Tower stair climb for charity and literally froze when I discovered that I was standing on the glass floor 342 meters (or 1,122 feet) off the ground. I literally had to be pushed off the floor by someone else because I simply could not move my legs. The fear is a very physical and a very real pattern for me. However, I have devised a strategy for Being fearless, which allows me to override this fear and access my courage, creativity and other resources that I need in that moment to solve my problem.

Believe me when I say that if I can reprogram my automatic default responses to fear and override my hardwired responses then anyone can. Here is an example of what I have been able to do. You can visit my website www.GinaML.com to see a short video of me Being fearless as I plummet more than 500 feet toward the ground in an exhilarating bungee jump in New Zealand. I'll never forget the feeling of being suspended in that river canyon and the view that I had. I had never seen a river gorge from that perspective before. I was struck with the realization that I had been offered a new perspective through my willingness to move through my fear.

By devising a strategy to overcome my automatic default response to heights, I was able to have a life experience that would never have otherwise been possible. This jump now acts as a reminder for Being fearless in all areas of my life because it reminds me of the incredible rewards that await me when I choose to expand, to grow and to learn. By the way, my legs still go weak when I hit the 10-foot-high mark, however my fear no longer has any control in dictating my actions or my happiness. The fear response is still alive and well, but my ability to override the response is what makes all the difference to me.

> *"You gain strength, courage and confidence by every experience in which you really stop to look fear in the face. You must do the thing which you think you cannot do."*
> *– Eleanor Roosevelt*

REMAINING POWERFUL

The real challenge that we face is our ability to remain powerful in the midst of crisis, adversity and failure. What is your conditioned response to crisis? What do you define as a crisis or stress? What is your pattern? We've already covered the fact that your initial reaction to a crisis or challenge is an automatic fight-or-flight response. Being powerful stems from the ability to override this response at the very moment that you become conscious of it and the resulting patterns that ensue from it. Being powerful means being emotionally self-aware and directing your responses instead of having them be directed by fear, default or hardwiring.

The amount of time that you remain in "crisis mode" is completely up to you. As I mentioned earlier, it is very easy to fall into a vicious cycle of crisis and reaction. First, there is the actual event that initiated your fight-or-flight response and then, in your heightened sense of awareness, you begin to notice more of what's wrong. This fires off another fight-or-flight response, which leads to more focus on what's wrong. And the crisis cycle has begun. The circumstances do not dictate when you will come out of this cycle. It is entirely your choice. When you realize that it really is your choice, then you will no longer be at the mercy of your circumstances.

CHOICE

I have developed a process that you can use to override your automatic default response in any challenging situation. I call it "The Simple Process" because it is just that: simple. There is one caveat to The Simple Process though, it's not always *easy*. If it were easy, then everyone would view crisis and challenge as opportunities and everyone would be able to override their automatic default responses, glean the learning in any situation, grow and move on enthusiastically to the next challenge. But, it's not easy because of the ultimate responsibility that comes with recognizing that it is eventually up to us.

It therefore comes down to a choice; your choice. This is what The Simple Process is all about. Because it is about choice, it is not always *easy*. There are pros and cons to every option. There always are and there always will be. But one thing is certain:

> "When we are no longer able to change a situation, we are challenged to change ourselves."
>
> – Viktor Frankl

our circumstances don't decide our happiness, our choices do. *It's not who happens to us but rather how we choose to respond to what happens that matters.* If you don't consciously choose your response, then a response will be chosen for you, either unconsciously by you or by accepting the prevailing response around. Either way, a choice is made.

Let's look back at our example of the child with the blocks. When her tower collapses, she actually has a choice in how she responds. She can throw a temper tantrum, hurl the blocks and blame them for falling down. Or, she can calmly assess the situation, notice the design issues and attempt to build the tower differently. Which choice do you think will lead to a more powerful and resourceful outcome?

You might be resistant to this way of thinking. That's okay—stay with it. It happens all the time in my seminars, with my clients and even in my own mind. We are often resistant to accepting responsibility for our happiness because it is scary.

I ask you to put this way of thinking on the shelf while you read this book. I'm not saying that you have to abandon your paradigm, but I am requesting that you merely suspend it while you consider a new paradigm. Think of it as trying on a sweater. You don't have to buy it, but it doesn't hurt to put it on and see how it fits.

It is scary to think that it is our choices that dictate our happiness. Accepting this responsibility means giving up our excuses, our reasons and our justifications. And that feels vulnerable. And vulnerable doesn't feel safe. But I offer that taking back the power from your circumstances is worth the "vulnerability" because the reward of getting your power back is the very thing you are trying to accomplish by attempting to control your circumstances.

Imagine if your happiness wasn't dependent on getting anything, changing anyone or eradicating any circumstance. Imagine if you could be happy regardless of what was happening to you. Wouldn't you be just a teeny bit interested in finding out how that might work?

> *"The important thing is not to stop questioning.*
> *Curiosity has its own reason for existing.*
> *One cannot help but be in awe when he con-*
> *templates the mysteries of eternity, of life,*
> *of the marvelous structure of reality."*
> *– Albert Einstein*

COMPANION **ONLINE** RESOURCE	💡	**THINK AGAIN!** Visit www.GinaML.com/Chapters to get a summarized version of this chapter for your quick reference.

CHAPTER TWO

～～～

THE FEEDBACK LOOP OF LIFE

"Evolution is chaos with feedback."
– Joseph Ford

This entire book is based on an important premise: everything in your life that happens to you is just feedback. At the most basic level, this means that you get out of your life what you are willing to put into it. Your circumstances will always reflect exactly where you are at in your life and what you are putting into it. The real power is learning how to interpret the feedback so you can use it to your advantage. Instead of judging your circumstances, you can learn to *assess* your circumstances so you can learn from them and leverage them to create a life that you love. Instead of having challenges and obstacles be a block to your happiness, you can learn to use these events as stepping stones to an even better experience.

At this point you might be asking yourself, "So what? What does that mean to me? How does that work?" Lucky for you that I happen to have a degree in engineering and did a thesis on feedback control loops. You see, if everything that happens is feedback, then you can use what happens as a tool to get exactly what you want. You can start to look at life as a giant feedback loop. I know that you might be cringing at such a scientific-sounding notion. Your reaction might be left-over negative energy from a science course that got the best of you. Not to worry. The feedback loop is actually quite easy to understand. A very simple definition is "a process that feeds back some of the output to the input of a system," and it looks something like this:

Basic Feedback Loop

As you can see, in a feedback loop, you can use the output to help alter the next input, thus achieving a more desired output the next time around. Using this same logic, wouldn't it make sense that you could use your undesired results (output) to help you change (input) so that you can actually get what you want (a better output)? Bingo!

A feedback loop always works in the same way, and you can use this understanding to help get what you want. You can use the information contained in your circumstance (output) to manipulate your next input so that your next output is closer to what you want. I call this process the "Feedback Loop of Life."

The Feedback Loop of Life

Life consists of a series of feedback loops. We want something (input), we do some behaviors (process) and we get an outcome (output). Sometimes we try to repeat the same loop over and over again, and other times we try only once. Basically, though, it's all feedback loops. Feedback loops all work the same way and are all governed by the same laws. Understanding how they work and the laws that govern them is the key to unlocking the secrets of getting what you want.

The classic example of a feedback loop is the thermostat. A thermostat has a desired set point for the temperature of the room. It is constantly monitoring the temperature. When the temperature falls below the set point, the thermostat tells the furnace to turn on. The thermostat uses the feedback to initiate a process to heat the room. When the temperature reaches the desired set point, the thermostat uses the feedback again to tell the furnace to shut off.

It is interesting to note in this analogy that the thermostat doesn't berate the furnace for not being on. Nor does the thermostat chide itself for failing to produce the desired temperature. The thermostat merely uses the information as a feedback to adjust the system to achieve the desired result. How often do we become upset at the circumstances in our life for being different from what we want? How often do we expect other people to change so we can be happy? Or worse, how often do we beat ourselves up when we fail? The answer in each case is, "we do it all the time."

When you accept the premise that everything is feedback,

you release yourself from being a prisoner of your circumstances because your outcomes are no longer judgment points. Your circumstances are nothing more than simple feedback; information that you can use on your journey to happiness. Consider this idea while you continue reading this book, for it may give you a fresh perspective on challenging circumstances, crises and failures. It may lead to the understanding that you can be happy regardless of your circumstances.

AN ENERGETIC VIEW OF THE UNIVERSE

Thanks to Einstein, we know that everything in the universe is energy in some form. His famous discovery of $E=mc^2$ changed the way all of life was understood. The theory of relativity forms the basis in which scientists have viewed our world ever since. Simply put, Einstein's theory states that any fragment of matter can be understood as an equivalent amount of energy (albeit expanded by a large multiplier). Likewise, all energy takes on a different form in the physical world. The universe is made up of both mass and energy and the two are interchangeable and convertible using Einstein's theory of relativity. Einstein once remarked, "We have been all wrong. What we have called matter is energy, whose vibration has been so lowered as to be perceptible to the senses. There is no matter." In other words, matter is just a term for "visible energy."

All energy is fluid, always moving into form, through form or out of form. The universe holds the potential energy for an infinite number of expressions in matter. True power derives from the ability to harness the unformed potential energy so that we can have what we want in our physical experience.

Taking this view of the world is essential in understanding the concepts and processes presented in this book. Everything is energy, including you and me. We are just a big bundle of energy vibrating at specific levels. The human body is the physical part of this energy and our thoughts and emotions are the invisible part. Thoughts and feelings are more

> "We are what we think. All that we are arises with our thoughts. With our thoughts, we make our world."
>
> – Buddha

than just biochemical reactions; they are actually electromagnetic patterns of energy. We emit energy every day in the form of thoughts and emotions. We transmit this energy into our physical worlds using our bodies through our behaviors. All energy in the universe is subject to laws that govern energy. One of the most useful (and most talked about) laws is called the Law of Attraction (LOA). But, it's not what you think.

THE LAW OF ATTRACTION

Let's start this conversation by focusing on what the law of attraction is NOT because there has been a lot of hype and controversy about the LOA in recent times. First of all, it is not as big a deal as everyone makes it out to be. It is not hard to understand. It does not negate God. It is not only for New Agers. In fact, the LOA is not new at all. *The New York Times* published an article on April 6, 1879 using the phrase "Law of Attraction."[5] It is not something you need to activate, nor is it something that you can opt out of. You are not required

---

5　　"To Leadville in Winter, Colorado's New Mining Camp." *New York Times*, April 6th, 1879.

to understand it or even believe in it in order for it to apply to you. The LOA is not magic.

Now let's focus on what it is. The LOA is a powerful way of understanding how energy flows. Einstein's theories suggest that the entire universe is just energy vibrating at different levels. Everything vibrates at a particular frequency. When something vibrates at a specific frequency, it naturally resonates with and attracts other things that have the same frequency. In other words, like attracts like. This is the Law of Attraction in a nutshell, and it applies to all energy in the universe. It is like two tuning forks; the vibration of one will subtly provoke vibration in the other until both vibrate together in harmony. And like a tuning fork, our thoughts and feelings emit specific energetic vibrations that externally resonate and attract frequencies that correspond to those vibrations.

> "Ask and it will be given to you; seek and you will find; knock and the door will be opened to you."
> – Jesus Christ

The Law of Attraction governs the way in which potential becomes reality. In others words, the LOA is a way of explaining how something that is visible (matter) developed from something that isn't visible (potential matter or energy). When it comes to how we can affect our results, the LOA allows us to understand how to transform our thoughts and feelings into the circumstances of our lives (the visible energy). I like to think of it as a series of energetic "reductions." As energy makes the journey into form, the vibrations must be lowered or reduced in order for us to be able to detect it with our senses and classify it as "matter." Our behaviors act as a bridge between the starting point and the ending point.

THOUGHT, FEELINGS, ACTIONS AND RESULTS

It is important to understand the mechanics that govern the process by which our thoughts and feelings create our results. Dr. Thurman Fleet was a chiropractor in the early part of the 20th century that developed a model for explaining this process. According to his model, the flow from potential reality (invisible energy) to matter (visible energy) is as follows:

Thoughts ⇨ Feelings ⇨ Actions ⇨ Results

The potential for something to exist begins in our thoughts, really in our imagination, as just that: a *potential* reality. It begins as an idea in our mind. Consider that everything there is began as an idea in someone's mind. This thought is then activated through our emotions. In a sense, an emotion is what strengthens the energy of a random thought. You may have heard some people define emotions as "energy in motion." We carry out actions that are consistent with our way of Being. These actions or behaviors are neurological patterns in our bodies that are linked to our states of Being. Finally, the behaviors lead to the manifestation of some type of result that appears in our physical reality (visible energy).

THE BACKWARDS PARADIGM

We have been incorrectly conditioned to believe that stuff

(people, places, things) can make us happy. How many times have you heard, "If I only had more money, then I could do what I wanted and then I would finally be happy"? This paradigm is called "HAVE–DO–BE." It's the way most of us approach our lives. And it's completely backwards. Recall that thoughts lead to feelings, feelings lead to actions and actions lead to results. But if we use the backwards paradigm of HAVE–DO–BE, then it would mean that results lead to actions, actions lead to feelings and feelings lead to thoughts. You can plainly see that this is backwards.

A more empowering paradigm is actually BE–DO–HAVE. Building on the previous diagram, let's see what happens when we map our new paradigm onto this flow:

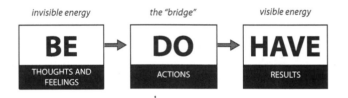

You can clearly see that it actually flows BE–DO–HAVE. It flows from the potential reality (invisible energy) to the physical reality (visible energy), and not the other way around. Consider that there is much wisdom in the saying, "money can't bring you happiness." But perhaps, happiness could bring you money? The physical result of money is actually the visible end of an energetic cycle. Here is another way to look at it:

The energetic cycle that governs your life, your experiences and your circumstances begins as energy in the form of a potential reality. It all starts with your "Being." Don't worry if you are confused by this, people often ask me to explain to them what "Being" means. In fact, I struggled with understanding it myself for many years. The opportunity lies in considering that a potential reality is just that: potential. It is a possible version of reality, but it's not actually Reality itself. This clarification is the basis for Being powerful in your life.

THE FEEDBACK LOOP OF LIFE

Let's have another look at the Feedback Loop of Life. All we have to do to have anything we want is to go back to the beginning of the process and make a shift. This is exciting! What makes it even more exciting is that if we do not get what we want the first time (i.e., we have a crisis, a challenge or a failure), then we can immediately use that feedback to inform our next input in order to generate a new outcome. We know exactly what to do because the answer is sitting right in front of us. Our results (or lack thereof) always give us useful feedback that we can use to change our version of reality.

THE FEEDBACK LOOP OF LIFE

In a feedback loop, the output informs and suggests a possible new input. In the BE–DO–HAVE paradigm, we must remember to go back to the beginning of the cycle if we are to truly impact the outcome. Ben Franklin said it first: "The definition of insanity is doing the same thing over again, expecting a different result." If we keep getting the same results, it means we haven't really changed what matters.

The other key distinction to notice within the BE–DO–HAVE paradigm is that our happiness is not dependent on getting <u>anything</u>. Happiness is a state or a mood and according to our diagrams, it is found at the beginning of the energetic cycle and is not dependent on the outcome. Your circumstances have <u>nothing</u> to do with whether or not you are happy. Your state (your happiness) is completely dependent on a combination of your thoughts and the feelings that you attach to those thoughts. Happiness is a choice and it comes from inside not outside. And, of course, we are not only talking about happiness. This also applies to the full range of emotional states, especially peace, love and joy.

> "Happiness resides not in possessions and not in gold, the feeling of happiness dwells in the soul."
>
> – Democritus

Throughout our entire lives we have been conditioned to

believe that in order to be happy we have to get *something*, be it fame, fortune, beauty or even spirituality. We have been continually told that the answer to our happiness lies "out there." WRONG! Happiness is a choice. If we are not happy, then we have chosen it that way. We have the power within us to be happy, no matter what is happening *to* us. In fact, we have the power within us to feel anything that we want to feel any time we like. We have been trained to abdicate this power to something beyond our control and have been conditioned to wait, hope and even pray for something to change on the outside so that we can finally be happy on the inside. Our lives merely reflect the choices we have made about ourselves. If we want to see something different in our lives, we first have to make a different choice.

Happiness is not a condition bestowed upon you by some other force. Circumstances don't make you happy or unhappy, but your choices do. Choice is a very powerful concept because it implies accountability and responsibility. We are all responsible for our lives, every single minute of them, regardless of what is happening to us.

In Roberto Benigni's *Life Is Beautiful,* the main character, Guido and his son are sent to a Nazi concentration camp where he maintains a positive state. As a result, his son has no idea where they are and continues to live his life innocently. How was it possible for Guido to remain happy while he was in a Nazi concentration camp? It was a conscious choice. His son never realized they were in a concentration camp because Guido protected his son's innocent model of reality. By choosing to maintain a positive focus, he saved his son's life. This is a powerful *choice*, folks. Some of the happiest people are living with the worst of circumstances, and some of the unhappiest people live in a world of unlimited privilege. Happiness is not circumstantial; it is a choice, plain and simple. Happiness isn't gotten; it's chosen.

CHOOSE IT OR LOSE IT

You might be saying, "Why on Earth would I NOT choose to be happy" or "Why would I choose to be unhappy?" It may sound insane to think that when you are unhappy you have chosen it that way. I don't know why and I can't answer that for you. There are a million reasons. I can tell you this though—your choice is being made unconsciously. If you are not choosing to be happy in the moment, then you are giving up your power to choose. A choice will be made for you. Often, we default to the general consensus of the people and circumstances that surround us. This is not a problem when times are good and everyone is in a generally positive state. However, when times get tough and people get down, then it is really easy to sink down with them. If you don't take responsibility for choosing your way of Being, then you will unconsciously choose the prevailing way of Being. Either way, it's a choice.

Over time, we have been trained to think that our happiness comes from something that happened on the outside. We were trained to think in terms of the HAVE–DO–BE paradigm. We have forgotten that we are the ones doing the choosing. Understanding the energetic cycle and the Feedback Loop of Life helps you to regain the knowledge that you have the power to choose. At any given time, you can choose your way of

Being. The choice needs to become conscious. The great news is that even if you aren't conscious of what choice you have made, your circumstances will always relay to you the choice that brought them into being. Your circumstances will always give you useful and accurate feedback.

BREAKING THE CYCLE

This brings us back to a main point of this book, which is how to be powerful when your circumstances are undesirable. Remember that your reaction to any threat is an automatic default stress response, which is designed to keep you alive during a crisis. However, our definitions of stress and threats have become so common that we perceive almost everything as a stressor, and this has led us to create situations of chronic stress. Staying in a stress response for long periods of time is detrimental to your health and well-being. Your long-term well-being depends on your creativity and problem-solving. It depends on your ability to reason, to learn, to grow. All of these things are virtually impossible when you are in a state of fear, doubt, worry or panic.

Fear, doubt and worry are states that bring into reality results that are consistent with those negative states. Namely, more crises, more challenges and more problems. The challenge we face is that once something goes wrong, we tend to focus our attention on what's wrong. We unconsciously direct our RAS to find more of what's wrong, which is unfortunate because our RAS is excellent at following instructions. This new information perpetuates our stress response and we enter the crisis cycle. The only way out of this cycle is to override your automatic stress response by initiating a state that will not feed the crisis cycle. You must change your focus. The hard part is doing this while you are in the midst of a crisis or a challenge. It requires conscious choice. It requires you to think in a different way.

THE POWER OF CRISIS AND CHALLENGE

Access to power is available for anyone in any crisis or challenge because everything that happens can be used as feedback. Every time we suffer a crisis, a challenge, a failure or a setback in our lives, we are being presented with very useful feedback to what is not working. The crisis can serve us by serving our growth. When used as feedback, failure can be the very best thing that could happen to us. It doesn't feel good. In fact, it never feels good, but it always serves us. This is the ultimate paradigm shift. When you can

> "I have not failed. I've found 10,000 ways that didn't work."
>
> – Thomas A. Edison

begin to view everything that happens to you as ultimately serving your growth and evolution then you will finally be free of suffering from your circumstances. This is the power of a crisis.

You are free to override your inclination to get sucked back into the cycle of crisis by using the feedback inherent in your circumstances to inform you on which choice you should make going forward. By making this choice, you will set in motion the energetic laws of the universe. When you make a change at the beginning of the energetic cycle, then you will ultimately see a different outcome. There will be a lag, however, because we live in a physical world and it takes time for a potential reality (energy) to become a physical reality (visible energy) through our behaviors. This is where faith comes

> "For those who believe, no proof is necessary. For those who don't believe, no proof is possible."
>
> – Author unknown

in handy. The dictionary defines faith as "belief that does not rest on logical proof or material evidence." You must have faith in the process.

A SIMPLE PROCESS

By using the Feedback Loop of Life in conjunction with your understanding of the way energy flows, you can literally have anything you want. You have to be willing to repeat the process over and over again, continuously feeding back your results until you have your desired outcome. This is not always as easy as it sounds. I said it was *simple* but not *easy*. Often, our results are hard to swallow because of the meaning that we attach to them.

The human mind is charged with the task of making sense of the world. It loves to create models of the world. In fact, it needs models to explain and understand the physical world. Therefore, the mind is always making up models and comparing the current situation against these models. This, in and of itself, is not a problem. The problem arises when we begin to believe that our models are the only reality or truth in the world. Remember our individual representations of reality are just maps and a map is just a representation of a place; it is not the place itself. It gets harder to apply The Simple Process when you bump up against one of your "truths." One of your biggest obstacles to real happiness is clinging to your model of reality as the only Reality.

"Simply the thing that I am shall make me live."

– William Shakespeare

COMPANION ONLINE RESOURCE	THINK AGAIN!
	Visit www.GinaML.com/Chapters to get a summarized version of this chapter for your quick reference.

CHAPTER THREE

BEING: THE POTENTIAL REALITY

"Often people attempt to live their lives backwards: they try to have more things, or more money, in order to do more of what they want so they will be happier. The way it actually works is the reverse. You must first be who you really are, then, do what you need to do, in order to have what you want."

– Margaret Young

"Being" is the most important concept in this whole process because it is who we are Being that drives the energetic cycle that manifests the results in our lives. Remember that we are human *beings*, not "human doings" and, as such, everything we experience is a result of who we are Being—not the other way around. Given that everything is energy, then it follows that you must go to the source of your energetic outcome if you are to produce a different outcome. You must go back to the beginning of the cycle where your outcomes exist as mere potential and examine that part of the cycle for the answers. In an ideal world you would always choose a powerful way of Being.

The concept of Being is not easily explained as I have learned over the years. In fact, I struggled with the concept for almost 15 years myself. You can allow yourself to be confused by the concept but try to remain open to it because it holds the key to having anything you want in your life. In the simplest terms, Being is really about the condition we are in during each and every moment, both from a psychological and physiological view. Some people call this our "state." Being is how we are operating in our reality. Being is who you are. I have used a capital "B" to signify it in this manner.

> "To be or not to be. That is the Question."
> – From William Shakespeare's Hamlet

WHAT IS REALITY?

To better understand Being, let's first take a look at the concept of Reality. Reality can be defined as the state of things as they actually exist. It seems a simple enough definition, but reality has been the topic of debate for ages. In attempting to determine what actually exists, we have discovered that it is hard to come up with a definitive answer. It used to be enough to say that if you could perceive it with your five senses then it actually existed. But we know that things like electricity and microwaves actually exist so that definition doesn't work. Then quantum physicists made it more challenging by showing us that things don't exist in absolute terms but rather in probable terms. From a quantum viewpoint, the likelihood that a basketball will appear as a basketball is high, but it's not 100 percent certain. Quantum physics suggest that there is always an element of uncertainty. Some scientists claim that Reality cannot exist independent of having someone to observe its existence. The topic of Reality has been debated from a spiritual standpoint for eons. Some schools of Buddhism state that Reality is something void of description.

The purpose of exploring Reality is not meant to confuse you but rather to illustrate that the concept of Reality is, in and of itself, confusing and ambiguous. The ambiguity in defining Reality is where the opportunity lies. What we call "reality" is actually a representation of what really happened so that we can make sense of it. Hence, Reality with a capital "R" means the actual event and reality with a small "r"

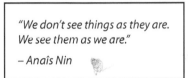

"We don't see things as they are. We see them as we are."

– Anaïs Nin

means your internal representation or *version* of Reality. The opportunity lies in the information that gets *left out* when we interpret Reality as our reality.

Recall from previous chapters that there are millions of bits of information that are available to you in every second and that your nervous system can only consciously handle about 126 of them. For the purpose of this book, those millions of bits of information can be thought of as Reality and your conscious mind can use only 126 bits to create what you call "reality." You can plainly see that your version of "reality" is a mere fragment of what is truly available in each and every second. Your reality is a representation of Reality, but it's not Reality itself; it is a map of Reality. The first characteristic of maps is its representation of a place, but it is not the place itself. In this context, it is easy to accept that many things can get left out of a map, perhaps even critical bits of information. The second characteristic of maps is that the map is only as good as the cartographer and the cartographer's tools. In this context, the map can be improved if the skills and the tools of the map-maker are improved.

YOUR INTERNAL REPRESENTATION

Neuro-linguistic programming (NLP) is the study of excellence and how to replicate it. NLP is a set of succinct techniques (models) extracted from therapeutic geniuses that help people *quickly and painlessly* overcome significant obstacles in their lives, thereby enabling them to discover valuable resources for getting what they want. I want to use the NLP model of communication to illustrate how Reality comes to be your reality.

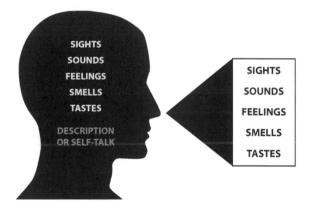

An external event in Reality comes into your nervous system via your five senses. It is easy to think of your five senses as the "input channels" for the external event. These are visual (sight), auditory (sounds), kinaesthetic (feelings/touch), olfactory (smells) and gustatory (tastes). The millions of bits of information available (per second) for your five input channels must be reduced to 126 bits so you can make sense of them. This filtering is done through a series of deletions, distortions and generalizations such that the end result makes up your internal representation (IR) of that event. In essence, this IR is your "reality."

Your IR mimics the external event in that it has the same following components: pictures, sounds, feelings, smells and tastes.

In addition to the above five qualities, your internal representation also includes another component: thoughts or self-talk about the event (how you describe the event in words).

Your IR is just that: internal. It takes place *inside* you. The important difference to note is that your IR includes an additional component that the "real" event did not include, which is the meaning or self-talk that you attached to it. This additional component is critical in understanding and controlling your response to your circumstances.

WHAT YOUR BRAIN DOES

The brain is a very complex part of the human body. One of the functions of your brain is to predict outcomes by continuously sorting, classifying and comparing events to determine where they fit in the models of Reality. Obviously, it is in your best interest that your brain does this as quickly and as accurately as possible for your well-being. For example, when you first learn that touching hot coals will cause a burn, your brain creates a model for that experience linking the hot coals to burns and pain. It is in your best interest that your brain gets really good at predicting whether or not you will burn yourself on hot coals because obviously burns hurt and cause damage to your body. Each time you burn yourself on hot coals will reinforce your model that hot coals will burn you every time.

World-famous brain researcher and neurosurgeon, Dr. Karl Pribram showed that past experiences help to build within us a set of familiar patterns which get established and maintained in the neural networks. Once a model of Reality has been established then your brain begins using that model to sort and classify events and to direct your behavior. The longer a particular model is used, the stronger the neural networks will become and the faster the brain will be able to sort and classify information based on that model. Most of the sorting and classifying that is done by your brain is not conscious to you since it happens so quickly and so habitually that you don't notice the process at all. You are just left with an external event and your resulting behavior while being unconscious to the process that determined your behavior. From our hot coals example, your brain will have made that process so efficient over time that you won't need to ponder whether or not you should touch the coals. You will just know that it is true that when you touch hot coals you will get burned. But, in actual fact, the behavior was an outcome of the model of reality that included a belief that hot coals will burn you every time.

I know that many of you are saying right now, "But that IS

true—hot coals will burn you *every* time." I chose this example for a reason because I know firsthand that this is not an accurate statement. In <u>my</u> version of reality, "Hot coals burn you *some-times*." I have had the opportunity to participate in a firewalk where I successfully walked barefoot over a bed of hot coals (1000°F+) with no burns whatsoever on my bare feet. Please don't go out and try this for yourself because it was an intensive training session in which we spent the greater portion of a day preparing for this test. However, I share this story with you to illustrate that even a statement as indisputable as "hot coals burn *every* time" is not *always* true. There was a very distinct sequence of events that allowed for the construction of a new model that enabled us to walk across those coals unharmed. It is important to illustrate that the successful outcome lay in the creation of a new model that actually included the possibility of the successful outcome.

The firewalk is a powerful example for understanding that, as humans, we erroneously perceive our internal representations to be true when they are merely one possible model of Reality. Some models are definitely better than others, but in the end, they are still only models. In an effort to be efficient, our brains often work with the same models so as to strengthen them and increase the probability that the prediction will be accurate. In that sense, your internal representation of an event determines your focus because your brain will continue to focus on that internal representation pulling data from your circumstances to support your claim. Recall the function of your RAS from previous chapters. The function of your RAS is to seek out and find information that supports your internal representation or model of the world. Your internal representation is what

> "The dissenter is every human being at those moments of his life when he resigns momentarily from the herd and thinks for himself."
>
> – Archibald MacLeish

instructs your RAS on what to focus on and what to discard. You will be able to find proof for whatever it is that you set your focus on because there is an infinite number of combinations when you are looking for 126 bits from the millions of bits in each second. Focus is determined by how you have chosen to see the world.

THE COMPONENTS OF BEING

Let's start with the description that Being is really our psychological and physiological condition in each moment. It is who we are. Some people refer to it as our "state." I find the term "state" confusing because it means different things to different people. In some schools it means just the emotions and it other schools it means much more. This concept is still too complex, so let's try and break it down into more manageable chunks. There are three main components that make up the way we are Being in any given moment. Your state of Being is made up of a mental, emotional and physical component. I use a triangle to represent Being because it implies that all components are intertwined and equally important. They cannot really be separated because they are coupled together. Every single state of Being has with it a mental component that is coupled with an emotional component that is coupled with a physical component. It's a package deal.

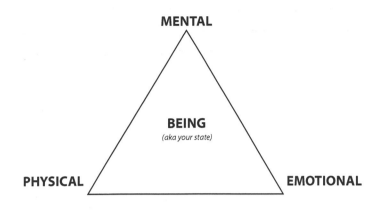

THE MENTAL COMPONENT

The mental component of your state of Being includes anything going on in your mind. This includes thoughts, self-talk and your focus. Focus is determined by your model of the world; how you see the world. What you focus on expands, regardless of whether or not it is positive or negative. This is a primary function of your RAS—to seek more of what you are focusing on. When you focus on what is wrong, then you get more of what is wrong. You may have heard the saying, "What you resist persists." Resistance is a form of focus; it is paying attention to something negative. By resisting something you are actually giving it attention and energy, which means that it will most certainly become an active part of your experience. Remember, your RAS filters out all but 126 bits of the millions of bits of information available to you in any given second. Re-

> *Whether you think that you can, or that you can't, you are usually right."*
>
> *– Henry Ford*

sisting something directs your RAS to focus on it, thus making it part of your reality.

If your goal is to get what you want, then you have to start by asking yourself, "What do I really want?" It is not enough to merely think about it. You have to create as complete a representation of it as possible such that it becomes your focus and your RAS starts collecting information that supports it. Recall that your internal representation of any event includes the following components:

- Pictures (visual)
- Sounds (auditory)
- Feelings (kinaesthetic)
- Smells (olfactory)
- Tastes (gustatory)
- Self-talk (thoughts or descriptions about the event)

It would make sense then that you should learn to describe what you want with respect to the above mentioned components. To describe it in any other way would be to create an incomplete representation. This distinction is where the biggest misunderstanding of the Law of Attraction occurs. Many people believe that you merely have to sit there and think or wish for what you want and it will somehow magically appear. Thinking about something is just one component of creating an internal representation and it is usually not enough because it is only 1/6th of the whole representation. This is why most techniques that simply employ positive thinking are not always successful. The reality is that you can think anything you want, but if you don't actually believe it (i.e. you don't create a complete representation of it) where it becomes real for you, then you can never experience it in your reality. The idea has to be congruent at all levels of your Being otherwise you will produce inconsistent or undesirable results.

According to Charlie Greer, "the National Science Foundation put out some very interesting statistics ... the average person thinks about 12,000 thoughts per day. A deeper thinker ... puts forth 50,000 thoughts daily."[6] If you are a deep thinker (and I'm sure you are because you are reading this book), then that means that roughly one thought

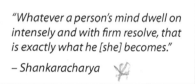

> "Whatever a person's mind dwell on intensely and with firm resolve, that is exactly what he [she] becomes."
>
> – Shankaracharya

per second is passing through your mind during your waking hours. In my seminars, I explain this by using the analogy of a stock ticker. Have you ever watched the stock prices fly by on the bottom of your TV screen? There are so many of them and they just keep rolling through. It's the same with your thoughts. They are just there, rolling through your mind. Thoughts only become powerful when you energize them by incorporating all of the sensorial components of the internal representation. Thoughts become really powerful when they get energized with emotion. The question is: are you consciously directing your thoughts and feelings or are they being directed for you?

6   Greer, Charlie. "What Are You Thinking?" *HVAC Profit Boosters, Inc. Newsletter.*

BUILDING A POWERFUL INTERNAL REPRESEN-TATION

When the external event (Reality) gets transformed into your internal representation it does so through a series of deletions, distortions and generalizations so as to filter out all but 126 bits of the millions of bits in each second. The big question when examining an internal representation is: what got left out? Or more importantly, what got left out that, if it were brought back in, would make this representation more powerful? This is one of the keys to creating a powerful state of Being—creating new models. If you create a new and more powerful model of Reality, then it will give you more choices for your behaviors, which will ultimately lead to more powerful results. Let's examine each process individually.

> "Our deepest fear is not that we are inadequate. Our deepest fear is that we are powerful beyond measure."
>
> – Marianne Williamson

Deletion is one process that our minds use when filtering out 126 bits of information from millions in each second. It is the process by which we only pay attention to certain aspects of our circumstances and ignore the rest. Essentially, we overlook or omit certain sensory information. The opportunity here lies in the fact that you can recover deleted information to build a stronger internal representation.

Distortion is essentially when we make things better or worse than they really are. Distortion occurs when we misrepresent reality in some way. Phobias are a good example of distortion because the person has distorted the external event or object such that it poses a heightened risk in their experience of it. The opportunity here is to remove the distortion and build a more robust and accurate representation of the external event.

The third process is generalization, where we relate things we are learning to our past experiences. At its best, generalization prevents us from having to learn something over and over again. At its worst, generalization is how we take a single event and draw global conclusions. When you remove the generalizations, then you are able to deal with each event individually allowing for unique qualities to appear. This makes your representation more robust.

It is easy to understand then how two people in the exact same circumstances could have completely different experiences. Every individual deletes, distorts and generalizes information from the outside in a totally unique way so that everyone ends up with a completely different internal representation.

When my son was little, he used to get random nosebleeds. It started when he was about two years old. By the time he was five, he was getting two or three nosebleeds per week. Most of the nosebleeds would happen at night. The other curious thing that started happening when he was five was that he started really freaking out when his nose started bleeding. He would require a lot of help to calm down and stop his nosebleed.

One day when he was drawing a picture, I asked him why he panicked every time he had a nosebleed since he was very accustomed to having them, knew how to stop them and it always worked out fine. He looked at me like I was nuts and said, "Because my heart pumps my blood and my heart is where my love is, so when I get a nosebleed then my love is coming out of me and I don't want to lose all my love." I was stunned. I considered that if this were *my* model of reality, then I would freak out every single time I saw a drop of my blood, too. His behavior made complete sense to me once I understood his model of the world. What a gift to be given such a clear view of his little five-year-old model. Once I helped him understand that this wasn't how it worked, he could correct his model and he never freaked out during a nosebleed again.

This interaction gave me firsthand knowledge of how our models dictate our responses and lead to our behaviors. I started to ponder how many other things he did that made complete sense to him based on his model of the world and how many parenting struggles that I had faced that were likely the result of differing models. What a gift. Our conversation ended that day with him asking one final question, "Does that mean that my smartness isn't really coming out when I blow my nose, too?"

THE PHYSICAL COMPONENT

The physical component can also be referred to as your physiology. We will use the term primarily to refer to body posture and movement as it pertains to your state of Being. When you change your physiology, your mind automatically follows suit because a change in your physiology will trigger a change in your biochemistry. Any change in your biochemistry affects your state of mind, which affects your behavior. You are familiar with the fact that ingesting things like food, drugs or alcohol can alter your biochemistry, which then alters your state. You can also change your physiology through movement or meditation or breathing, as any one of these actions has a biochemical reaction. This biochemical reaction is what sets the stage for your state of Being.

Changing your physiology is the fastest way to effect a change in the way you are Being. Think of all of the muscles in your face that are associated with smiling. Simply smiling has been shown to instantly lift your mood thus allowing you to focus on options that were previously unnoticed. In a sense, changing your physiology allows you to access a different model of the world, which gives rise to more choices.

Recall from Chapter 1 the powerful biochemicals associated with inner peace include endorphins, serotonin, dopamine and anandamide. When these biochemicals are being produced by our system, then we are easily able to direct our attention to what is right in our situation thereby activating our RAS to seek out and find more evidence of what is going right. These chemicals do not get produced in optimal quantities in our system when we are operating in a depletion mode, such as a stress response. They do get produced when we are functioning in a renewal mode and there is adequate time for the body to attend to the ongoing maintenance and repair that is essential to our well-being.

Therefore, in order to change our physiology such that these desired biochemicals can be present in greater quantities, we need to increase the amount of time that we spend in responses that provide renewal and less time in responses that cause depletion. This means we need to minimize our stress response as much as possible to allow our physiology to operate in peak form thus allowing us access to peak results. We need to get better at controlling our responses to situations such that we can maintain a positive response that doesn't place any added burden on our system.

THE EMOTIONAL COMPONENT

Some people refer to emotions as feelings, but they are more than that because they include both a physiological and psychological component. Some emotions bring us empowerment whereas others limit our potential. Happy, sad, depressed and motivated are some examples of emotions. There are many emotions. In fact, some emotions are combinations of others. Let's start with the basics.

BASIC EMOTIONS

There are many different emotions that a human being can experience and it can be overwhelming to try and identify all of them. For the purpose of this book, they will be grouped together into four main categories:

i. Passive Positive Emotions—such as peace, serenity, contentment, compassion

ii. Active Positive Emotions—such as love, joy, excitement

iii. Active Negative Emotions—such as fear, anger, anxiety

iv. Passive Negative Emotions—such as apathy, sadness, hopelessness

There are many hormonal correlates and shifts that emotions set in motion—and the hormones then reinforce the feeling of the emotion and add the texture of the feeling. The emotions in each of the categories have commonalities when it comes to the levels of adrenaline, cortisol and DHEA in our systems. As well, the emotions can be organized according to which part of our autonomic nervous system is stimulated—whether it is the *fight-or-flight* liabilities of our sympathetic system or the *rest-and-digest* benefits of our parasympathetic system. This diagram, from HeartMath Institute, maps the most common emotions onto two different axes.

The horizontal axis represents the system in your body known as your hypothalamus-pituitary-adrenal (HPA) axis. Recall from the earlier chapters that this system is what regulates the levels of the hormones cortisol and DHEA in your system, and that the ratio of the two is most indicative of well-being. When levels of cortisol rise too much in relation to DHEA, then your system is in a phase of depletion. On the opposite side, when levels of DHEA rise and act as a buffering agent to the effects of cortisol, then your system is in a phase of renewal.

The vertical axis represents your autonomic nervous system (ANS). When your arousal is high (as in an attack or an exciting activity) then your body is primarily in a sympathetic nervous response and the level of adrenaline in your body is high. Likewise, when the arousal level is low (i.e., resting) then you are primarily in a parasympathetic response and there is little or no adrenaline being produced in your body.

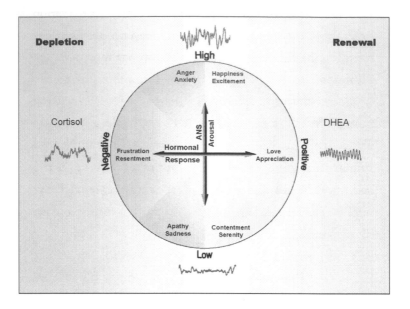

© HeartMath. Reprinted with permission of the
Institute of HeartMath

i.   Passive Positive Emotions

With passive positive emotions such as peace, serenity and contentment, the body is operating primarily in the parasympathetic nervous system. The body is undergoing a renewal of resources. The levels of both adrenaline and cortisol are low and the levels of DHEA are high. This combination allows the body to heal and make any necessary repairs and maintenance. The body is also able to produce the optimal levels of desired biochemicals such as endorphins, serotonin, dopamine and anandamide which allow us to feel calm and happy.

These emotions are called "passive" because they exhibit a low level of physical and emotional effort and low levels of adrenaline. These emotions are the highly sought-after relaxation states that we strive for in meditation, prayer or rest. In these states, our daily lives feel effortless and we are more aware of the flow of life.

My friend, Ingrid Bacci has written a wonderful book called *The Art of Effortless Living*. In her beautiful book she outlines concrete strategies for living your life effortlessly and joyfully. The main message in her book is that you first need to be aware of the benefits of living effortlessly and then recognize that you are the one with the power to choose this path. We'll cover some of the basic ways to choose these passive positive emotions towards the end of this chapter.

ii. Active Positive Emotions

With active positive emotions such as love, joy or excitement, the sympathetic response has been stimulated resulting in an increase in adrenaline. This provides the energy necessary for activity. The levels of cortisol remain low and the levels of DHEA remain high. You are able to carry on higher energy activities without depleting the body of valuable resources, provided that you do not maintain this state continuously. If too much adrenaline is continuously produced, then the overproduction could lead to a stress response and an inherent rise in cortisol.

These emotions are called "active" because they exhibit a higher level of activity—they are not passive emotions. Energy for this activity is provided by the increased levels of adrenaline in the body. These emotions translate our highest purposes into action in our real lives. People who operate in these emotional states are easily able to translate their core values and passions into results in their lives.

iii. Active Negative Emotions

In active negative emotions such as fear, anger or anxiety, the body has switched to a negative stress response. The levels of adrenaline are high in this sympathetic response. The levels of DHEA begin to decline whereas the levels of cortisol begin to increase. This cortisol/DHEA ratio has been linked to well-being and you want to keep this ratio as low as possible. When cortisol levels begin to rise and DHEA begins to fall then the body falls into a depletion mode whereby you are now using more resources than you have. This depletion can begin to take a toll on your health, especially if you maintain these states for long periods of time.

These emotions are called "active" because they exhibit activity—they are not passive emotions. Energy for this activity is provided by the increased levels of adrenaline in the body. The negativity of these emotions is related to the cortisol/DHEA ratio as well as the sympathetic nervous response. Remember that when you are in a sympathetic nervous system response, your body's ability to produce desirable biochemicals is greatly reduced thus leading your emotions in a negative direction.

iv. Passive Negative Emotions

Finally, in passive negative emotions such as apathy, sadness and hopelessness, the body is operating in a low level of arousal. Levels of adrenaline have dropped because high levels are not sustainable. Cortisol levels have also dropped due to the inability to continuously produce these hormones. Your body's ability to produce desirable biochemicals is also diminished. This leads your emotions further down the path of negativity.

These emotions are called "passive" because there isn't enough adrenaline to cause activity or action. The declining levels of hormones would suggest that the adrenal glands are simply unable to produce them. This is sometimes referred to as "adrenal fatigue." It often occurs when the adrenal glands have been continuously producing adrenaline and cortisol without adequate levels of rest and renewal.

WHERE DO YOU SPEND YOUR EMOTIONS?

Which categories of emotions dominate your experiences?

REGULAR DAY:_____

STRESSFUL DAY:_____

TRAFFIC JAM:_____

FIGHT WITH LOVED ONE:_____

READING THE NEWS:_____

THE CHICKEN OR THE EGG

Many people, including me, misinterpret the HeartMath diagram at first glance. We erroneously assume that it is the level of hormones that give rise to the emotions. However, this is not the case. According to Dr. Rollin McCraty of the Institute of HeartMath, the emotions are what direct the physiological response. He says that it is actually the emotions that cause the body to respond and not the other way around. This means that if we can get control of our emotional responses, then we can increase our physiological well-being. Are you starting to see where this is going? Choosing an optimal emotional response means you will have optimal physiology from a hormonal standpoint. Remember that all of the desirable biochemicals of peace are associated with positive emotions. Given that the physiology and emotions are always coupled with an internal representation or a focus, we are more likely to have positive representations of the world available to us when we are in optimal emotional and physiological states. This will lead to better results.

> "The greatest obstacles to inner peace are disturbing emotions such as anger, attachment, fear and suspicion, while love and compassion and a sense of universal responsibility are the sources of peace and happiness."
>
> – The Dalai Lama

PEAK PERFORMANCE STATES

Peak state refers to a situation when an individual is performing at or feeling their best. Other terms that describe peak state include "in the zone" or "in the groove." I've been able to recognize my own peak states as the ones where I have completely lost track of time because I was so consumed with what I was doing. The term "peak state" actually has its roots in the branch of psychology known as Humanistic Psychology that was heavily influenced by Dr. Abraham Maslow in the 1960s.

Maslow popularized a term known as "peak experiences," defined as "especially joyous and exciting moments in life, involving sudden feelings of intense happiness and well-being."[7] The peak experience is uplifting; it releases creativity and allows the individual to see many opportunities. He believed that everyone was capable of peak experiences and those who do not have them somehow depress or deny them. Maslow's thinking was that we should learn how to identify these states and cultivate them with conscious awareness to increase our quality of life.

> *"We can have in life but one great experience at best, and the secret of life is to reproduce that experience as often as possible."*
>
> *– Oscar Wilde*

Many years ago, I experienced an intense peak experience. I had just come out of a very serious relationship and my heart was broken. I was in a relationship with a man whom I really loved. There was nothing obviously wrong, but it just didn't work out. I suffered a broken heart at the end of that relationship. I made a commitment to myself that I would not engage in another relationship until I sorted out what had gone wrong; what I had done wrong and why didn't he love me? I did a lot of soul-searching, reading and thinking. I discovered that I didn't really love myself. In fact, I wasn't sure I even liked myself. Was it even possible? I had no idea.

This question led me to take a vacation to the West Coast of Canada. I had always been drawn to the mountains and the sea. On this particular vacation, I had the chance to go to Whistler, British Columbia to do some skiing. I was skiing with a very good friend of mine on a particularly brilliant day. The sky

---

7   Maslow, A. *Religion, Values and Peak Experiences.* New York: Viking, 1970.

was so blue it was blinding. They actually have a name for this type of day at Whistler—it's called a "Bluebird Day." We had stopped on the side of a run to take a break and take in all of the beauty around us. All of a sudden, it hit me like a cosmic two by four, right out of the blue (pardon the pun), and I had an overwhelming feeling that everything was perfect. Everything, including me! I was filled with a sense of peace, love and joy all at the same time. I realized that there was nothing wrong with my last relationship because it helped me to become conscious of how I felt about myself and to uncover some important resources that I needed. I realized that the problem wasn't that he didn't love me (in fact I am sure that he did), but that the problem was that I didn't love myself. All this time I thought that I *needed* someone to love me, but learned that I just needed to give that to myself. I had one of those moments that you simply cannot explain to another person. I turned to my friend and said to her, "I don't need anything; I already have everything I need." It was amazing. And then it was gone, although something had irreversibly shifted deep inside me. I had a glimpse of who I really was, and I was really happy with what I had seen. A deep knowing settled into my heart at that moment. Now, I didn't *need* a relationship, but that didn't mean that I didn't *want* one.

Interestingly enough, within hours of finding that love for myself within myself, I was introduced to my soulmate. It was undeniable from the moment we shook hands. Yet, the circumstances were not as obvious; here was this complete stranger and I'm thinking to myself, "I'm going to marry this guy." Huh? Even I have to admit, it sounded crazy, yet I just knew. What I didn't know was that he had felt the exact same thing when he shook my hand but felt even crazier for thinking it. Needless to say, we were engaged after spending only 18 days together living at separate ends of the country. I learned a powerful lesson about following my heart and intuition at that time.

What I realized many years later was that I had experienced a peak experience on that mountainside at Whistler. The result that came out of that peak experience was incredible in that it instantaneously led me to the most enriching relationship of my life. It appeared as a miracle because the time it took to go from a potential reality to a physical reality was very short. As soon as I incorporated my newly found resources and shifted my belief about myself, then my circumstances automatically reflected this new paradigm. I began to realize that amazing results were correlated to peak experiences, and now that I had a blueprint for the experience I could begin to recognize it, cultivate it and choose it on a more regular basis.

THE DIVIDING LINE

Intuitively, we know that there are emotional states that are positive and ones that are negative. My interest in this topic led me to read a fascinating book called *Power vs. Force* by Dr. David R. Hawkins. In his book, Dr. Hawkins shares his methodology for defining and calibrating levels of consciousness. He shows how every emotional state is correlated to a certain level of consciousness. Wouldn't you know that the most positive emotional states correlated at the highest levels of consciousness? Likewise, the most negative emotional states correlated at the lowest end of his scale. The following diagram gives an interpretation of his work to illustrate the relative power of the emotional states.

The emotional states that lie above the dividing line correlate to the same emotional states that have beneficial physiological impact as we saw in the HeartMath diagram above. It seems that choosing these emotional states not only directs your physiology in a positive way but also indicates your relative level of consciousness and, hence, power. When you choose an emotional state that is above the line, you are operating from a position of power. When you choose an emotional state that lies below the line, you operating from a position of force. Force equals stress, and stress activates a stress response (fight or flight). The best way to avoid a stress response is to choose a positive emotional state above the dividing line.

THE WESTERN CONDITION

I have observed that most people in Western cultures tend to live in a state of chronic low-level stress. This is not the full-fledged version of an attack that would cause you to run away or stay and fight but rather a lower level version of stress that keeps you in a negative state of depletion on an ongoing basis. There is little or no time spent in a state of renewal for your body to catch up on the repairs and maintenance necessary for optimal health and wellness. People who attend my seminars have heard me jokingly refer to this as "Western-itis."

Think of it in terms of the example of a saber-toothed tiger attack. If you turned around and saw a saber-toothed tiger running at you then you would respond in a full sympathetic fight-or-flight mode and do everything in your power to escape the danger. This response would end once you reached safety. At this point your body would switch back to the parasympathetic system so it could replenish the resources used up in the sympathetic fight-or-flight response. This is how we were designed to work—mostly in resting states with bursts of activity. With "Western-itis" there is no saber-toothed tiger coming at you, however you are plagued with the thought that he *might* attack you, so you are constantly looking over your shoulder in anticipation of danger. It is the *thought* of the tiger that keeps you in a state of chronic low-level stress, thus overusing your sympathetic nervous response and depleting your system of valuable resources for no *real* reason. If this response occurs over an extended period of time, then you also suffer the effects of increased cortisol and lowered DHEA.

We were never meant to maintain a constant stress response. We were meant to allocate adequate time to resting and replenishing. This is the basis for many ancient resting rituals such as the Jewish Sabbath or the day of rest on Sundays in the Christian faith. Not only were these days intended for spiritual renewal, but also for physical and emotional renewal as well.

The sympathetic system is more akin to a sprinter who needs to stop and take a rest once the race is finished. If not, there will not be enough resources left for the next race.

DO YOU OVERREACT?

Write down any situation that you think you might overreact in. Be conscious of where you have the opportunity to choose a different response.

_____

_____

_____

_____

CHOOSING POWERFUL STATES OF BEING

The most effective way to consistently produce powerful results in your life is to ensure that you start with a powerful state of Being. Regardless of your circumstances you <u>always</u> have the power to choose your state of Being, however you might not always be conscious of having a choice in each and every moment. This is a profound distinction because it has the power to turn any seemingly powerless moment in your life into an opportunity for you. Your personal power in any situation is directly related to how well you recognize your power in choosing your response. Rest assured that if you do not make a conscious choice, then a choice will be made for you. It will be either be an unconscious choice with respect to your past experiences, or it will be related in some way to the prevailing default state of the people around you.

A powerful state of Being is made up of powerful mental, physical and emotional components. Choosing a powerful mental component means focusing on what is right instead of what is wrong. It means choosing a complete powerful representation of the world that includes a lot of choices and possibilities, as well as directing your thoughts and self-talk in a positive way. A powerful physiology is one of strength and alertness, which includes standing up straight and being centered and grounded in a way that feels strong and flexible. A powerful emotional state is a positive state of renewal, whether it be peace, love or joy. When you make the conscious choice to embody a powerful state of Being, you allow for your neurology to create powerful behavior. This will ultimately lead to powerful results.

The opposite is also true. When you choose negative states of Being (whether conscious or not), you are setting in motion a limited choice of behaviors that will lead to less than desirable results. It's that simple.

ANCHORING

Wouldn't it be great if you could just push a button and get into your most powerful way of Being? You can and these buttons are called "anchors." An anchor is any stimulus that is associated with a specific response. Anchors can happen naturally or they can be deliberately created. The purpose of intentionally creating an anchor is to have the response easily accessed by the trigger. Anchoring is an effective way to store and recall powerful states of Being so that they are available to you when you need them. An anchor can be visual, auditory and kinesthetic. Tastes or smells can also be anchors. Real estate agents use this principle when they recommend that you bake fresh cinnamon buns just before the open house because many people associate the smell of cinnamon buns with comfort and satisfaction. The smell of cinnamon buns will influence the people at the open house such that they will be operating from a more positive state of Being and are more open to seeing what is right with your house.

It is very easy to create an anchor for a state of Being. Let's say that we want to create an anchor for being joyful and that we want to use the first knuckle on our left hand as the location of this anchor. Anchors are most effective when they capture the state of Being as it occurs naturally. In this case, you would remember to press your left knuckle each time you were experiencing joy. Perhaps when you were laughing with friends or happy to see someone. Each time you would press your knuckle. Over time, pressing your knuckle would allow you to access this state of Being without thinking about it consciously, as the anchor would have become part of the neural network associated with that state of Being.

Another way to reinforce this anchor would be to intentionally create a joyful state of Being by recalling a past experience of it. The key to making this technique work is to ensure that the memory is as vivid as possible and that it includes all aspects of the internal representation of that state of Being including what you saw, what you heard, what you felt, what you smelled, what you tasted and what you said about it in your head at the time. It important to this process that you are looking through your own eyes when you recall the experience versus seeing yourself in the picture. Once you have revisited all of that then you would apply the anchor when the joyful state of Being was at its strongest point or at its peak.

A third way to create an anchor is to construct a state of Being by building what you think would be a good representation of it. This is not based on past experience but rather on an educated guess of what you think it would be like. Again, it should include all components of the internal representation in order to make it as real as possible. Again, ensure that you are looking though your own eyes when you build this experience. This technique for creating anchors is the least effective because there is no past experience with the state of Being.

ANCHORS AWAY

Create an anchor for yourself right now.

Step 1: Choose the state of Being that you want to anchor (e.g. Calm).

Step 2: Recall a time when you remember Being Calm. Close your eyes and see the images in your mind. Make sure you are looking through your own eyes as if you were reliving the moment right now. Notice the sights, sounds, smells and tastes. What feelings are present in your body? What thoughts are present in your mind?

Step 3: As you feel the experience building to a peak, press the anchor.

Step 4: Hold the anchor until the experience starts to decline and then release the anchor.

ACCOUNTABILITY

Regardless of what is going on in your life, you are always a human *Being*. You either choose your state of Being consciously or unconsciously. Either way it is still a choice by you. Consciously choosing your state of Being means that you deliberately set your mental, physical and emotional states. Choosing your state unconsciously means that you allow outside circumstances to direct your mental, physical and emotional states without recognizing that these components are always under your control. Often, these unconscious states of Being are undesired states like fear, doubt or worry.

When we find ourselves Being fearful or doubtful or worried, we feel powerless. The tendency is to blame the circumstances for this powerlessness. We tend to look to the outside for the cause as well as the solution to this problem. We do this because we sometimes forget that our state of Being is always under our control. In any moment, you can have access to all of your personal power by choosing to deliberately create a powerful state of Being.

> "First we make our habits, then our habits make us."
> – Charles C. Noble

Being accountable for your results does not mean that you are at fault for everything that happens in your life. Instead, it means Being accountable for the way you have chosen to respond to your circumstances. The circumstances will never be in your control and trying to control them is a futile and stressful endeavor. Better you learn early on how to maintain command over the one thing that you can: your choice to be the best possible version of yourself in any given moment.

THE POTENTIAL REALITY

Discovering who you are Being is the first step in the cycle that brings your results. From an energetic standpoint, this portion of the cycle is also known as the *potential* reality. This *potential* reality is one possible version of Reality but it is not Reality itself. There are an infinite number of possibilities for what Reality might be. When you choose your state of Being, you are selecting <u>one</u> potential possibility from this infinite list. In a sense, you are putting your flag in the ground and taking a stand that this is the way it is (for you). Your life, your results and your circumstances will reflect this choice that you have made whether you have made it consciously by declaring it or unconsciously by allowing your past experiences and programming to determine who you are. The fact remains: when it comes down to who you are Being, the choices available to you are infinite. The question is: What choice are you going to make? Will it be conscious, powerful and full of opportunity or will be it unconscious, based on the past and predictable? Will you think for yourself anew or will you sink into an old pattern? The choice is yours.

> *"Be the change that you want to see in the world."*
> *– Mahatma Gandhi*

COMPANION ONLINE RESOURCE	**THINK AGAIN!** Visit www.GinaML.com/Chapters to get a summarized version of this chapter for your quick reference.

CHAPTER FOUR

～～～～～～

DOING: THE TEMPORARY REALITY

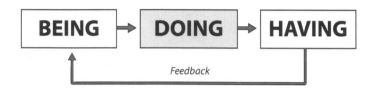

"Do...or do not. There is no try."
– Jedi Master Yoda, The Empire Strikes Back

The middle section of the Feedback Loop of Life is related to our behavior. It focuses on what we do. Recall from the previous chapter that the state of Being is what determines behavior. These behaviors then determine our outcomes. It is the most tangible part of our physical existence and often it is therefore perceived as the *only* part of our existence. We have now seen that it is not the only part of our existence. In fact, if you spent most of your time consciously choosing a powerful state of Being then the "doing" part of your life would feel rather effortless and fluid. Gone would be the days of struggling to get through the day. You would have flow because your behavior would flow from your powerful choice. These mechanics are neurological in that your state of Being is transmitted through your neurology to produce action using your body.

These actions produce your results.

Once you have chosen a powerful state of Being or a powerful response to a situation, then you must begin to take action that is congruent with this choice. This means being able to tell when an action is and isn't right for you. This also means that you need to learn to trust that what happens along the way is always in service of achieving your outcome. It might not always feel like it, but if you have been deliberate in choosing a powerful state of Being, then the most straightforward path will always present itself in accordance with that choice.

> "Fall seven times. Stand up eight."
>
> – Japanese proverb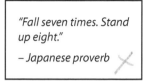

This path might include obstacles that are in need of resolution in order for you to reach your destination. You can handle any obstacle as long as you remain conscious of your response to the obstacles. Are you going to let them take you out or are you going to use them as the stepping stone to your success? Again, as always, the choice is yours.

You are probably starting to notice a theme by now. It always comes down to choice. You always have the power in every second of every day to make a choice. We often forget that we have this power, and in forgetting, we often give up our power to the circumstances, whether they are people or events. The great news is that as soon as you stop and think about your ability to make a choice, you get all of your power back. The rest will flow from that.

Regardless of where you are in your life, you can begin today to take actions that will bring you closer to what you want. Assuming that you have identified some powerful ways of Being in the previous chapter, let's begin to look at some processes for moving towards your successful outcomes. We must begin with the end in mind.

WHAT IS YOUR FINISH LINE?

What is it that you actually want? Most people don't know the answer to this question. Yet, knowing what you want is highly correlated to getting it. Many people have heard the story about a study that was conducted at Yale about whether or not the graduates of 1953 had specific goals. In the story, it was shown that the 3 percent of people who had written goals were earning 10 times as much as the ones who did not have written goals. Many people have heard this story. It has also appeared as a 1979 Harvard study. Apparently, it is a myth according to a December 1996 issue of *Fast Company* magazine. They couldn't find any proof of existence of the 1953 Yale study. However, the controversy inspired a group of researchers led by Gail Matthews at Dominican University of California to conduct a study of their own. Their findings were not surprising. Having clearly written goals was significantly correlated to achieving them.[8]

In her study, Dr. Matthews randomly assigned participants to one of five groups:

- Group 1 was asked to simply think about the business-related goals they hoped to accomplish within a four-week block and to rate each goal according to difficulty,

---

8   Matthews, Gail. "Gail Matthews Written Goal Study Dominican University." Dominican University.

importance, the extent to which they had the skills and resources to accomplish the goal, their commitment and motivation and whether they had pursued the goal before (and, if so, their prior success).

- Groups 2-5 were asked to write their goals and then rate them on the same dimensions as given to Group 1.

- Group 3 was also asked to write action commitments for each goal.

- Group 4 had to both write goals and action commitments and also share these commitments with a friend.

- Group 5 went the furthest by doing all of the above plus sending a weekly progress report to a friend.

At the end of the study, the individuals in Group 1 only accomplished 43 percent of their stated goals. Those in Group 4 accomplished 64 percent of their stated goals, while those in Group 5 were the most successful, with an average 76 percent of their goals accomplished. "My study provides empirical evidence for the effectiveness of three coaching tools: accountability, commitment and writing down one's goals," Matthews said.

In my seminars or my private practice, I always say that if you don't know where you are going then you will never know if you get there. In a sense, you will spend your life going somewhere and nowhere at the same time. I always advise my clients, whether they be personal or corporate, to determine what it is they actually want and then write it down. We don't just write it down in any old way, we use a very specific process that I have developed to allow them to start with the big picture and work it down until they have a manageable list of things to do. It all starts with a vision.

VISION—THE BIG PICTURE

You might be confused by the term *vision* because everyone out there has a different definition of the word. Mine is simple: A vision is literally something you *see* in your reality. In that sense, it is an outcome; an experience. You must have a clear vision for what you want. A vision is really "big picture." Think of it as the umbrella under which all of what you really wish and hope for can reside. Your vision is what drives your life. Most people have never thought this big before.

Vision is the biggest way that you can describe what you want. You can do this in all areas of your life or you can have just one. A powerful vision will push you way beyond your limits. The most powerful vision is a mega-vision: one that you cannot even hope to achieve in this lifetime. What?!? The reason for this is twofold: first, if you have no expectation of achieving this mega-vision, then you will be free to attempt to create it in as many different ways as possible, and second, when your mega-vision is huge, it can inspire and include others with similar visions. The greatest leaders of the world have huge mega-visions that enroll others and take years and years to come to fruition. Think of Martin Luther King Jr. or Mother Teresa. Their visions were not small. You need to

> "Let the beauty of what you love be what you do."
>
> – Rumi

think big! Your vision will guide you when you are trying to determine whether your actions are right for you. Your vision is directly correlated to who you really ARE. Now is the time to ask yourself, "What do you really want to experience?"

✝ WHAT DO YOU SEE?

- Close your eyes and start to create your personal vision.
- What do you see for yourself?
- Look around. Describe the situation. The more detail you can describe (in the present tense, please), the more vivid your vision will become.
- Use all five senses: What do you see, hear, taste, smell and touch?
- What does it feel like in your vision? How does your body feel in your vision?
- What do you see as possible for this world? What matters to you?

GUIDING VALUES AND PRINCIPLES

The other components that will direct your actions are your guiding values and principles. It is all well and good to know what your finish line is when you have the luxury of thinking about your life as a series of isolated events. But in actuality life is dynamic and always changing. It is very helpful to know what it is that guides you so that as life happens to you at breakneck speed, you can act accordingly. Values are a set of statements that help guide your direction when you arrive at a crossroads.

Take a moment to consider what you value. For example, I really value kindness in relationships. It is very important to me to be kind to others and for others to be kind to each other and to me. A guiding value is something you feel strongly about and are willing to take a stand on. It is also something that will help you decide whether you should do something or not.

You should also define your principles. Principles are more specific than values because they encompass detailed instructions on how you will live your life (how you will BE). They usually include multiple values along with guiding actions in specific circumstances. For example, at Critical Pathfinders, the corporate team-building company that I co-founded with my husband, we have a strategic framework that includes the following principles (obviously there are many more):

- Our work is fun!
- We are dedicated to making this world a better place!
- We focus on the solution, not on the problem!

Values, principles and your vision are the big picture of who you are. They don't change much over time and they act as the umbrella over all of the actions in your life. If you take the time to contemplate who you are, what you really want and what you stand for in your life, you will find that you take away most of the uncertainty in your life. It's not that you don't know the answers to these questions. It's just that you probably don't know them *consciously*. Being conscious of what drives you is the key to understanding how to make the best decision for you in each moment. Think of it this way: your vision, values and principles are like your personal tour guides in this journey. They help guide you in the right direction. Now, it's time to get specific. Where do you want to go?

PERSONAL INVENTORY

What do you value in each of the following categories of life? What's important to you?

FAMILY:_____

CAREER:_____

HEALTH:_____

SPIRITUALITY:_____

PERSONAL GROWTH:_____

SOCIAL INTERACTIONS:_____

GOALS

We all have goals. Some are big, some are small, but everybody wants something at some point. A goal is simply something that you want but don't have *yet*. Even if we aren't conscious of our goals, we still have them. Making them conscious increases the probability of achieving them. Having a good plan also increases the probability of achieving them. The more clearly you define what you want, then not only are you more likely you to get what you want but also more likely to be able to recognize that you got it.

This process works, for people as well as businesses, because it is independent of the content. It doesn't matter what you want. The process of breaking it down is what matters. Let's start with your Big Picture; your vision. The first thing you should do is to break it down into four or five chunks. These chunks are basically your goals. They are directly related to your vision and they represent the first layer of action in achieving this vision. It helps to think of your vision as a finish line and your goals as the paths that lead to that finish line.

> "Go confidently in the direction of your dreams! Live the life you've imagined."
>
> – Henry David Thoreau

I have developed a technique that ensures your goals are robust enough to get you from A to B. I call it the SMASHing system and I have used it for hundreds of clients and seminar participants to help them increase their probability of success in getting anything they want in life. This system works for any goals, anything at all that you want in your life.

SMASH stands for:

Sustainable

Measurable

Actionable

Single-Minded

Harmonized

Sustainable

Is your goal capable of being sustained? Sustainable

goals are goals that are realistic and reasonable within the time frame expected. This isn't an opportunity to negate your ability but rather a checkpoint to determine if you are within reason of achieving your goal.

Measurable

You must be able to assess whether or not you achieve your goals. In a sense, your goals are mini finish lines along your path. These mini finish lines are only valuable if you can quickly ascertain your success by measuring against a benchmark or set point. Your goal must include some type of metric. This metric will provide useful feedback as to whether or not you got what you wanted.

Actionable

To be actionable, a goal must contain a verb. In other words, you must clearly define what you will DO with your time. Goals that lack verbs do not direct you to definitive action. You would be surprised at how many goals do not include a verb. For example, a client once told me that she wanted a perfect body by the time she went on vacation. There is no verb in her goal so it is unclear. A better way to state her goal would be to say "I will lose 10 pounds before my vacation". The verb in this goal is "to lose" and it is clear what needs to happen now.

Single-Minded

Your goals must have clarity of purpose. Too often, I meet people whose goals are wishy-washy and vague. They are not compelling and, as a result, rarely get achieved. Think about the difference between saying "I want to have more money" versus saying "I will increase my earnings by 50 percent by the end of the year." Having a clear purpose provides you the impetus for action. We will talk about breaking down your goals into manageable chunks a little later in this chapter. If you can't make your goal single-minded, then it is probably an indication that it is too big.

Harmonized

Your goals absolutely must be harmonized with your guiding values and principles. If you are out of alignment in this area, you will experience great difficulty in your day-to-day actions. Remember, the point is to continue moving towards the finish line. Therefore, your goals must be in harmony with your overall finish line.

The SMASHing system ensures that the actions we take are congruent with our finish line. It also allows us to take small measurements along the way to determine if we are on track in the big picture. There is always a most straight-forward path to our finish line and our goals act as the sign-posts on this path, helping us to understand if we are moving in the right direction.

SMASH IT

WRITE YOUR GOAL:_____

_____

_____

Rewrite segments of your goal to include the following components:

SUSTAINABLE:_____

_____

MEASURABLE:_____

_____

ACTIONABLE:_____

_____

SINGLE-MINDED:_____

_____

HARMONIZED: _____

_____

MAKING BABIES

One thing that stops a lot of people is that they become completely overwhelmed by the sheer size of their vision or goals. If from time to time you find yourself in this group, it may be helpful for you to learn how to make babies of your goals. This is the process of breaking down your goals until you feel comfortable with their manageability. The ultimate size of the goal is different for everyone, but the process is the same. First and foremost, all babies must pass the

SMASHing test. Second, the sum of the babies must equal the larger parent goal. The process is easiest to define using a simple example that most people can relate to.

Parent Goal—A New Year's Resolution: To eat a healthy diet by July 1st

First, we need to ensure that our parent goal passes the SMASHing test. Assuming that the goal is made on New Year's Day, it is definitely sustainable. It is reasonable to assume that a new habit could be installed in six months. The date of July 1st gives it a measure. The verb "to eat" is definitely an action. The goal is focused and single-minded and is harmonized with the individual's commitment to lead a healthy life. However, the goal is still overwhelming because it really isn't clear exactly what to do on each day between now and July 1st. Making babies will help clarify the goal and make it more manageable.

Baby Goals:
- To eat 10 servings of fruits and vegetables every day
- To reduce soda pop consumption to 1 can per day
- To limit sugar consumption to parties and special events
- To eat only organic food

Each of the baby goals passes our SMASHing test, and together they easily add up to a healthy diet. This could be the final breakdown of goals in this situation. However, if any of the baby goals still feel overwhelming, then another round of making babies can occur. This has a cascading effect in that each generation of goals can be broken down into more and more babies until you are literally left with a daily action plan of things to do that are direct descendents of your big-picture finish line. This is a great way to ensure that you are moving towards your finish line in the best way you know how. When you are ascertaining whether or not a baby goal is sustainable in the SMASHing system, you need to keep in mind how many generations of goals you have made. A baby goal might be sustainable in the 1–2 day mark if all the other goals in that generation are of that stature. In our example, you could make another generation of goal babies in this way:

New Parent Goal:
- To reduce soda pop consumption to 1 can per day

Next Generation of Babies:
- Reduce current soda pop consumption to 3 cans per day by April 1st
- Refrain from drinking any soda on the run to discourage "take-out" consumption
- Drink sodas made with real ingredients
- Replace at least 75 percent soda pop consumption with water or herbal tea

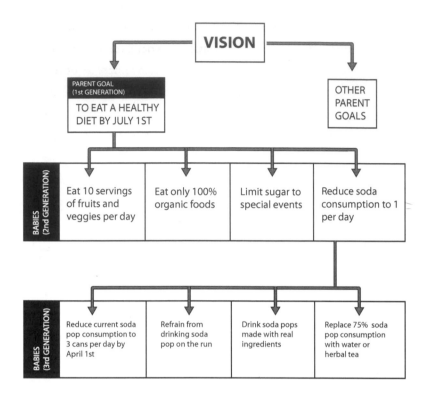

You can plainly see how each generation of goal babies gets more and more specific and easy to accomplish. In this way, you are able to take on even the biggest goals and break them down until you feel comfortable with the action plan. The next thing you can do is transfer this action plan to your daily calendar.

INSPIRED "TO DO" LISTS

It is possible to fill each and every item on your "to do" list with an action that is inspired directly from the big picture of your finish line. Making goal babies is an excellent way to move confidently towards your finish line. You must start at the very top with a clear and concise picture of your finish line. Then, you begin by making the first generation of goal babies. I recommend limiting each generation to four or five babies; otherwise, the plan gets too diluted. It can take as many as four to six generations of goal babies to get down to the tactical level of action lists. You will know it when you get there.

Once you are at the generation of the "to do" list, you simply transfer your action items to a 12-month calendar. I recommend using a 12-month calendar because many of your actions will be recurring (daily, weekly, monthly) and it helps to lay the whole thing out so you can see the path you have created. Once you have filled in the entire 12-month calendar with all your little goal babies, you will see that you have finally removed all the guesswork from life. Your calendar dictates exactly what you should be focusing on and when you should be doing it because it came directly from the big picture of your finish line. Gone are the days of dragging your feet and feeling overwhelmed by all your goals and the things you have to do. Your babies do the work for you by keeping you in line with your big picture of what you want. The final step in making goal babies is to start doing the actions immediately and with enthusiasm.

CAUTION

It is very easy to overlook the things that support you in achieving your dreams. Things like rest, relaxation and rejuvenation are as important as any official item on your action list. You must also include these types of actions in your 12-month planning calendar so you can see when you will recharge your batteries and ensure your energy levels remain adequate to do the things you want to do. I have a client who literally schedules every book she reads, every run she takes and even how many social functions she will attend every month. In this way, she is able to keep a balance between living the life of her dreams and maintaining a high enough energy level to reach the finish line. Obviously, life doesn't always go according to plan, but *having* a balanced plan is the key to understanding the give-and-take nature of your actions. Having a good plan allows you to feel confident in the actions you are taking every day because you understand exactly how they fit into the big picture of your dreams.

THROWING IT AWAY

Now throw all of this away. What? How can I suggest throwing the whole plan away after you spent so much time crafting it? Well, I'm not suggesting that you throw the plan itself away, but you must—and I stress MUST—throw away your attachment to it. You will inevitably become attached to your plan because you have labored to create it. You have spent a lot of time checking the "SMASH-ability" of your goals and rigorously readjusting them. You have spent a lot of time making the perfect babies and ensuring that absolutely nothing gets left out as you move towards the big picture of your finish line.

It is important to consider that while your way may be very well thought out, it is not the only way to achieve your outcome. There are a multitude of actions and behaviors that can also bring about success. This is a very important point to remember. Your way is merely one way, but it is not the *only way*. Being attached to your plan will prevent you from seeing the signs and hearing the whispers as to where you need to alter your course along the path to your goal. You must maintain your ability to see things as they are when they are happening. You have to stay present.

BEING PRESENT

I used to detest the section in any self-improvement book about being present. I never fully understood the term "present." In the past few years, I have come to understand it in a very powerful way. Hopefully, this

> "You evolve not by seeking to go elsewhere but by paying attention to, and embracing, what's in front of you."
>
> – Anonymous

distinction helps you too. Being present means being aware of what is *actually* happening in the moment that it is actually happening. Remember we can only really handle 126 out of millions of bits of information so we never actually experience *all* of it. We literally cannot. The first part in being present is recognizing that we are only ever seeing a *portion* of Reality. But that's not the nugget. The key to being present is what happens *inside* our heads once we make an internal representation.

The capital "R" Reality includes sights, sounds, feelings, smells and tastes that make up the complete experience. We filter this information down to 126 bits and add one additional component—our description about what is happening. This is sometimes referred to as our "internal dialogue" or "mind chatter." When we represent our experience internally and bring it into our own consciousness, we add a *description* about the event. The addition of this description is not actually part of the event. Moreover, the description usually has nothing to do with the event itself but rather is based upon past experiences. Remember that your mind's job is to sort and classify experiences according to the models that it has created. It is always matching or mismatching your experiences to determine whether this experience is a threat or a pleasure. Your internal description is not based on what is happening in the present moment; it is based on what happened in the past.

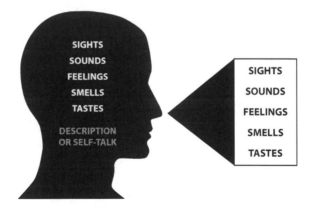

Therefore, being present means learning to quiet your internal dialogue and resist the urge to attach a description to what is happening. Being present means being aware of what is *actually* happening versus paying attention to your *description* of what is happening. Remember that you only get 126 bits of information per second and your self-talk or mind chatter takes up some of the bandwidth. If you can learn to reduce your mind chatter, then you will have more of your attention available to focus on what is actually happening. When you are present to what is actually happening then you have the power to direct your behavior based on the actual facts instead of allowing your behavior to be directed by a past response. Being present allows you to be flexible as you move towards your finish line. Being present is the key to remaining unattached to your plan.

FOLLOWING YOUR HEART

When you are present to what is actually happening in your life, it is much easier to determine whether or not it is in alignment with your guiding values and principles. It is much easier to make a decision about which way you should go when you understand where you *really* want to be going. You are not the same person that you were ten years ago, last year, or even yesterday. Doesn't it make more sense that your behaviors result from what is actually happening versus something that happened in your past?

Everything you do should be aligned with what is in your heart. That doesn't mean that every experience should be easy and pleasurable. But knowing that what you are doing is an expression of who you really are and what you really love should help to make every experience meaningful to you. When you are taking on a challenge or completing a mundane task, you should be fueled by the knowledge that everything you do is leading you toward your finish line. This knowledge will also be a source of strength when you are faced with a crisis or a failure. Knowing that you are on your *right* path will help you reframe any challenge that appears before you as an opportunity to move closer to your finish line. In a weird sense, the challenges lose their power because they are part of the process of moving toward your finish line.

READY, FIRE, AIM

I had an engineering professor who used to tell us "ready, fire, aim" when we were attempting to solve a difficult problem. He used to urge us to go with our gut instincts in solving a problem, test it out and finally determine if it actually worked. His basis for making this statement was that we were more likely to succeed if we took action right away instead of sitting around trying to find the perfect way to do something. He ascertained that even if we didn't get it right, we would have picked up a clue or an indication of what to try the next time. This process of trial and error served me very well in my engineering studies because it always led me to correctly solve more problems than I initially thought I could. This approach pushed me past my preconceived limits. It became a permanent part of my problem-solving strategies long after I graduated.

> *"Security is mostly superstition. It does not exist in nature, nor do the children of men as a whole experience it. Avoiding danger is no safer in the long run than outright exposure. Life is either a daring adventure or nothing."*
>
> *– Helen Keller*

Take action! Set your sights and then take action. Don't worry if you don't have all the answers. Don't worry if you might look foolish. Take action! It's the quickest and easiest way to determine if you are on the right path. Remember that in the Feedback Loop of Life all of your results are just feedback. The more feedback you get, the more complete your model will be. Your goal then should be to collect as much feedback as you can. This means trying things many times to see where they lead. If you follow the process in this chapter, you can feel confident that your actions will be aligned with your ultimate vision. Your actions will be organized and congruent with your values and guiding principles. Taking action without a plan can feel scattered and overwhelming, which is why most people shy away from taking action. However, when you have taken the time to figure out what you want and some possible ways to achieve it then taking action is merely an experiment. You must take action if you ever want to get anything in your life. You can't just sit there and hope that it will fall on your head.

THE TEMPORARY REALITY

There is a difference between taking *random* action and taking *inspired* action. When you take actions that cascade from what you really want in life, then you will be able to find joy in the most unusual places.

It is important not to lose sight of the fact that in the energetic cycle this middle section we call "doing" is a temporary reality. It is not forever. Once you initiate the cycle by choosing a state of Being then the temporary reality is where you play out this choice. Eventually these behaviors will lead to an outcome: a physical reality. The actual outcome isn't as important as how it reflects your state of Being that started the whole process. The temporary reality is a veritable playground where we get to test out different ways of Being and determine which actions feel most congruent with who we really are.

"I think of life itself now as a wonderful play
that I've written for myself ... and so my purpose
is to have the utmost fun playing my part."
– Shirley MacLaine

COMPANION ONLINE RESOURCE		THINK AGAIN!
		Visit www.GinaML.com/Chapters to get a summarized version of this chapter for your quick reference.

CHAPTER FIVE

~~~~~~~

HAVING: THE PHYSICAL REALITY

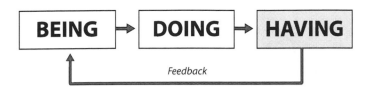

"Accepting, allowing and interacting with your life as though it is exactly as it should be, without making yourself wrong (or right) for what you discover, is the way to Self-Realization."

– Arial Kane

This segment of the book is dedicated to helping you understand how much power you actually have in <u>any</u> circumstance. It is not the circumstance that causes suffering but rather the response to the circumstance. With this realization, a new power can be found; a new world of choices opens up in the face of any circumstance. Contained within these new choices is the possibility of peace, joy and love, regardless of what is going on in your world.

It is helpful to classify circumstances into two categories. Firstly, there are the circumstances that are the results of our own behaviors and actions. These are *personal* circumstances. Then there are the circumstances that are completely out of our realm of control. These are *global* circumstances. Interestingly enough, we don't use this distinction to edit our responses to circumstances. Our responses are usually indistinguishable between personal and global circumstances. We tend to respond to what we see on the outside whether we have any influence over it or not.

The principles of this book apply to both types; however, in each case the circumstances are reflecting two different things. Personal circumstances are the outcomes of our own personal behaviors. These outcomes are the end of the cycle and reflect who we were Being. On the other hand, global circumstances can be viewed as being the *collective* outcome of the behaviors of a group of people. In this context, global circumstances reflect the collective state of Being of the group of people involved. In either case, the outcome always reflects the state of Being that produced it. For the purposes of simplicity we will use personal circumstances and personal outcomes to illustrate the principles in this chapter, recognizing that we can easily apply these principles when thinking about global circumstances or outcomes.

BLACK OR WHITE

Your outcomes are pretty straightforward to understand. You either got what you intended to get or you did not. There is no middle ground. You either get it or you don't. The perspective that will liberate you is that in either case you <u>always</u> get *feedback*. You always get an indication of how well your strategy worked. There is no guessing. Either your behavior produced the intended result or it did not. Your outcomes merely indicate whether your neurology was in alignment with your thinking. Inconsistent results indicate an inconsistency in the model that produced them. This is incredibly useful feedback and often goes completely unnoticed and unutilized. This happens mainly because we have been

> *"We learn wisdom from failure much more than from success. We often discover what will do by finding out what will not do. And probably he who never made a mistake never made a discovery."*
>
> *– Samuel Smiles*

conditioned to use our outcomes as judgment points instead of assessment points. We have been conditioned to use our outcomes to determine our self-worth. We often spend so much time judging whether we are a good person or a bad person when we evaluate our outcomes that we miss the point completely.

Even if people do get some useful feedback from their outcome, they usually try to utilize the feedback by manipulating their behavior. In this sense, they only go halfway back in the cycle and try and affect a different outcome. By failing to go to the source of the cycle, they create a situation whereby they will likely produce the same result despite hoping for something different. This is a frustrating and often futile effort because behaviors are the results of states of Being. If you don't go back to the source of the behavior, then you will meet with little success in creating a new and different outcome. Remember that the definition of insanity is doing the same thing over and over again and hoping for a different result.

So, we're back to this: you either get it or you do not. Now, instead of using this outcome as an opportunity to judge yourself, see it for what is really is: completely unbiased, nonjudgmental objective feedback. Once you have this feedback then you have the power to use it to inform you as to exactly what state of Being led to the behaviors that produced this result. If you are unsatisfied with your result, then you must change your state of Being. Whether you decide to change who you are Being is entirely up to you. It is your choice. When you realize that you always have the power to choose who you are Being then you will finally understand that the power in any situation always lies with you, which means that you don't need anything to change for you to get it.

DEBUNKING "BAD" RESULTS

We love to classify things. Remember, our mind's job is to sort, classify and make sense of the world. There is no reason why it would stop this process when it comes to our results. We have been conditioned to sort our results into "good results" and "bad results." Not only is this process harmful to our sense of well-being, but it is also useless. The word "bad" is not a definitive quality. Rather, it is very subjective and dependent on the individual definition of "bad." Let's try to unravel the word. The dictionary definition of the word "bad" is "having undesirable or *negative* qualities." Next, let's define "negative." A dictionary definition of "negative" is "having the quality of something harmful or *unpleasant*." A search on the word "unpleasant" leads to a definition as "disagreeable to the senses, to the mind, or feelings." Bingo! "Bad" is not a definitive term as it is subject to the input from your mind, senses and feelings.

If your results ultimately disagree with your model of the

world, then they get classified as "bad." Perhaps the problem isn't in the circumstances at all. Perhaps the problem lies in the fact that your model of the world is only one *possible* model of the world. This particular model of the world is the cause of the pain because using it leads to disappointment and suffering when evaluating your results. This is great news. You don't have to change a thing in your circumstances in order to rid yourself of the negativity associated with your results. You just need to choose a different model of the world.

So, where does that leave us when it comes to our results? If we no longer need to classify our results as "good" or "bad" due to their subjectivity, then we are finally free to see our results for what they really are: feedback. We can finally take an objective view of our results and begin to utilize their inherent learnings to make our lives better. From this point forward, "there are no bad results, only feedback."

EXPECTATIONS

Another source of suffering as a result of our circumstances is our expectation of how it was supposed to turn out. Having expectations is a serious cause for disappointment. If your actual outcome does not match your expected outcome, then the automatic default response is some form of disappointment, suffering or shame. Remember the effect of negative emotions on your body's internal systems. Whenever you find yourself in negative emotional states, you are putting your

> "The real voyage of discovery consists not in seeing new landscapes, but in having new eyes."
> – Marcel Proust

body under undue stress whether or not you have chosen the emotion consciously. By understanding that it is your expectations and not the circumstances themselves that cause the disappointment, then you can finally begin to take control of your thoughts and emotions. This is how you get power back from powerless circumstances: by accepting responsibility for having an expectation and for choosing to empower that expectation. The moment that you decide to disempower your expectations and choose another (more appropriate) response you will find that new choices and possibilities are available that were not visible before you changed your response.

From time to time, people cut me off in traffic. This used to upset me because I held the expectation that no one should *ever* cut me off in traffic. It used to really bother me. One day it dawned on me that the reason it was bothering me was because I was engaging in my expectation. I shifted my expectation and, miraculously, the other drivers stopped bothering me, even though they continued to cut me off! I realized that I can't control them, only my reaction to the situation.

100–ZERO

Another way to express this new view is to live life at 100–zero, where you commit to giving 100 percent of your effort at all times while expecting absolutely nothing in return. This is particularly powerful in relationships. You give 100 percent to the relationship and expect zero percent in return from your partner. If your partner is also living this way, then she or he is giving you 100 percent while expecting zero percent from you. It is a complete win-win situation with both partners giving and receiving perfectly. Think about your own relationships. Do you give 100 percent or do you hold back because you expect the other person to give or do or be something for you? Do you expect things from others and then

> *"Men [and women] are disturbed not by the things that happen, but by their opinion of the things that happen."*
>
> *– Epictetus*

get frustrated when those things don't materialize? We need to recognize that it is simply our expectation that is causing the upset, not the actual circumstances. It is *always* the expectation.

THE SOURCE OF MEANING

Believe it or not, you are actually the source of all of the meaning in your life. The meaning that you attach to any event in your life is generated in your mind as a way of sorting, classifying and explaining your experience. It is completely dependent on your own internal representation of Reality. This is why two people can experience the exact same thing and derive a totally different meaning from the situation. A different model equals a different meaning. This is a very powerful distinction. In fact, it is so powerful that many people have difficulty accepting it. People like to believe that meaning is universal and that everyone *should* believe the same things about certain events. These people believe that the meaning is an indisputable quality of the circumstance in the same way that color or sound might be an indisputable quality. However, that presupposition is entirely false. Meaning is something that gets attached once the external event gets internalized. Meaning happens in the internal representation of the event, not in the actual event itself.

Recall that the external event can be made up of sights, sounds, feelings, smells and/or tastes. This event gets processed by coming into your neurology via your five senses. In this process of internalization, most of the information actually gets deleted, distorted and generalized so that you can make an internal representation of the outside event using about 126 bits per second. When the event becomes internalized, the resulting representation includes sights, sounds, feelings, smells and/or tastes *plus* the addition of a description of the event as your mind tries to make sense of it. This description is the meaning. In your mind, this description is part of the event, but in Reality there is no such quality. Meaning is created internally and is not an inherent or an indisputable quality of the actual event.

The meaning that we attach to each event is subject to many different factors that shape our overall model of the world. These include things like values, beliefs, attitudes, memories, language, habitual patterns and decisions. Some of these factors are conscious such as your beliefs and some of these factors are completely unconscious, meaning that they occur outside of your conscious attention, such as many of your habitual patterns. The more conscious a factor is in determining your model of the world the easier it is to change it, thus changing the overall model.

Consider that the meaning that we attach to our circumstances is the source of most of our dissatisfaction and unhappiness. Mismatched meaning is also the source for most of the conflict in the world today. Consider how many wars are waged based on "truth." If our meaning-creation is an unconscious process then our resulting response to this meaning is also unconscious. When a process is not conscious, then there is no power in the situation because it runs outside of your awareness. When you become consciously aware that the meaning to which you have given the situation is the actual cause of your disharmony, then you finally have the ability to get your power back. All that is required is to make a different choice for the meaning you have attached to the situation. There are always multiple stories that describe the exact same event.

Imagine meeting a friend for lunch. You are waiting at the restaurant and your friend is late. Instantly, your mind creates a meaning about this event. Let's say your mind decides that your friend is late because she doesn't value your time. This makes you angry, and now you feel slighted by your friend. The longer you wait, the more upset you become as your mind spins this elaborate story. Have you ever done this? Of course, everyone has. By the time your friend arrives, you can barely contain your upset. Upon arriving, your friend apologizes and explains that she stopped to help an elderly lady carry her groceries and this caused her to be late. Not only was your meaning inaccurate, it also did not serve you or your relationship.

One thing you can do when you notice that you are upset is to recognize that you have created the meaning in the situation. The meaning is part of your internal representation and not actually part of the experience. The first thing to ask yourself is: "Do I know for *sure* that this is true?" You will usually find that you cannot be 100 percent sure that your explanation is the only possibility. If you find yourself stuck for an alternative, try making up some different explanations to account for the exact same event. For example:

- **Silly explanation**—Your friend was late because her trapeze practice ran late.

- **Dramatic explanation**—Your friend was late because she rescued a cat from a burning building.

- **Magical explanation**—Your friend was late because her unicorn had to eat before flying her over.

- **Touching explanation**—Your friend was late because she was reading a story to children at the local day-care.

- **Inspiring explanation**—Your friend was late because she was marching in a peace rally.

Once you have compared the five possible explanations and considered the possibility of each one, you should be able to see that there is no "truth." This should illustrate that your version is also not the truth and you now have the power to unchoose your meaning. You can detach from the meaning and get back into living your life, being happy in the present moment exactly as it is happening.

THE MIRROR PRINCIPLE

Consider that everything you experience in your model of the world is really a projection of your own perceptions. This is not a new theory. During the early part of the 20th century Carl Jung said, "Just as we tend to assume that the world is as we see it, we naively suppose that people are as we imagine them to be. In this latter case, unfortunately, there is no scientific test that would prove the discrepancy between perception and reality. Although the possibility of gross deception is infinitely greater here than in our perception of the physical world, we still go on naïvely projecting our own psychology into our fellow human beings. In this way everyone creates for himself a series of more or less imaginary relationships based essentially on projection."[9]

What Jung is saying is that we can only experience other people to the extent that we perceive it ourselves. Until we are aware of this dynamic, then we will tend to assume that the qualities belong to the other person, object or circumstance in question. By experiencing negative emotional responses to certain people or events to such great extents, we have refused to acknowledge the possibility that those qualities exist in us as well. Jung referred to this aspect as the "shadow" archetype. Jung's "shadow aspect" is a part of the unconscious mind made up of repressed qualities such as weaknesses, shortcomings and instincts. According to Jung, this aspect of you tends to turn your own negative personal qualities into a deficiency in someone else.

I am going clarify this section a little further because Jung and his theories were quite complicated. Let's take an example of someone who cheats on his/her taxes. Many people might conclude that this person is deceitful. According to Jung, the judgers are projecting their own deceitfulness onto the person who cheats on his/her taxes thereby disowning this quality. Now, it doesn't mean that these people are deceitful or should change their behavior to

---

9   Jung, C.G. *General Aspects of Dream Psychology* (1916). Also in CW 8: *The Structure and Dynamics of the Psyche*. P.507

be deceitful. Rather these people need to accept that they, too, have the ability to be deceitful. That it is a quality that is in them as much as anyone else. The difference is that we need to recognize that we have the power to choose to BE that quality or not. It is always a choice. There might be a situation where it would be totally appropriate to be deceitful. I'm sure the many women and men who provided safety and shelter to the slaves in the underground railway or to the Jews of Nazi Germany would tell you that it was a good thing that they were able to be successfully deceitful. By accepting all of the qualities within ourselves, we expand the breadth of behavioral choices that we have in any given situation.

> "I have learned silence from talkative, tolerance from intolerant and kindness from the unkind. I should not be ungrateful to those teachers."
>
> – Kahlil Gibran

Our lives are mirrors of our inner worlds. Everything that you experience in your circumstances is an indication of what is going inside of you in the same way that a mirror merely reflects the qualities of the object being reflected. I want to point out that everything that you experience is <u>not your fault</u>. Rather, the way in which you react to what is happening is driven by your own perception of Reality. In other words, you are not to blame for what happens. However, you are responsible for the way in which you respond to what happens. It is important to recognize the source of your experience as being your response to what happens. If you change your response, then you change your experience.

Imagine waking up one day with really bad hair. You can see how bad your hair is by looking in the mirror. Now imagine that you start yelling at the mirror and demanding that it shows you different hair. Your upset is coming from your expectation that the mirror should display the reflection as you want to see it. Under this expectation, you get upset and blame the mirror for continuing to reflect your bad hair. Obviously, the only way to change the picture in the mirror is to actually do something about your hair. Recognizing that the mirror is a reflection of reality gives us the freedom to choose. You can choose to fix your hair, thus also changing the picture in the mirror, or you can choose to do nothing about your hair, recognizing that the mirror will continue to display your bad hair. Either way, the choice is yours and there is much freedom in understanding this choice.

This principle applies to the rest of life in exactly the same way. In the Feedback Loop of Life, what we *have* is "the mirror." So, in your life, what you have on the outside is a reflection of who you are *Being* on the inside. If you are unhappy with what you see in your life, then it is absolutely futile to try to change something on the outside. You must go to the source of the image (who you are Being) and change it on the inside; then you can look to the reflection to determine if your change was adequate. You must look to the reflection for feedback on the changes you have made on the inside. If the reflection is what you want, you have succeeded; if the reflection is not what you want, you simply need to look to see what is out of place and then go inwards to change it.

In my workshops, I have actually given every participant a little mirror to remind her or him of the simplicity of the built-in feedback mechanism available to each of us at all times. By looking at life on the outside, in the mirror, we can determine what needs to be changed on the inside to alter the picture we are seeing.

USING THE MIRROR PRINCIPLE

This technique is so simple and allows you to change virtually anything in your life. Here's how to use it:

1. Identify what is causing you to be upset.

2. Change your language to "I."

3. Resolve the issue and change the way you are Being.

1. Identify the Upset

It is easy to spot the cause of your upset—it is the one thing you want to change or the circumstance (or person) you want to eliminate. It is usually the thing you blame for your life not being the way you want it to be. You typically place this blame on something external. For example, you might find yourself saying, "If only my boyfriend treated me with respect, then I would be happy." It is obvious to you that your unhappiness is the fault of your boyfriend and something he is or isn't doing. Now, however, you have to shift into realizing that he doesn't cause you to be unhappy. *You* do. Or better put, the *choices* you make are causing you to be unhappy. Your boyfriend is simply a reflection of your inability to treat yourself with respect. In other words, don't shoot the messenger! Instead, you need to be grateful for the clarity you are being shown.

2. Change Your Language

This is very powerful. By changing your language to "I" you are taking responsibility for your own upset. This gives you the power necessary to change your energy. In the example above, changing your language means that your statement becomes, "If only I would treat myself with respect, then I would be happy." Notice that the onus is now on you to change your behavior. There is no longer anyone else to blame for your situation. You now turn your focus inward, where it is possible to recreate and change the picture that is being reflected in your mirror.

3. Resolve the Issue

Once you have refocused the responsibility back on yourself, you are finally able to resolve the real issue. When you change the language to "I" then ask yourself, "How does this make me feel"? The emotions that arise during this process are important clues to resolving the issue. Chances are that these (usually negative) emotions are the very things that are preventing you from developing new behaviors and hence different results. This may be simple or challenging depending on what the issue means to you and how deep it runs within you. Remember that your mind has created this story to protect you from some perceived harm, so it may be challenging to reverse the belief. However, the power once again rests with your choice. You can choose to delve deeper into the issue and look for the answer, or you can choose to ignore it and turn the other way. Delving deeper might mean you need someone's help to see it a different way. Perhaps a friend, therapist, parent, minister or health-care professional could help shed some light on your issue. Don't be afraid to ask for help in resolving any issues that you uncover. The negative emotions are not serving your growth, but they are an indication that essential learnings are available from past experiences. When you get the learnings from your past challenges the negative emotions will likely disappear.

MIRROR MIRROR

1. Identify what is causing you to be upset. Look for people or situations that cause you to be upset. _____

_____

_____

2. Change your language to "I." In the statement above, re-place all references to others with references to yourself in the first person. _____

_____

_____

3. Resolve the issue. List three different ways you can re-solve the real issue. What new choices do you have? _____

_____

_____

PAY ATTENTION TO WHAT GETS YOUR ATTENTION

The easiest way to determine what part of your reflection isn't working for you is to notice what gets your attention. Note that what gets your attention might not get someone else's attention. Whatever it is, you are noticing it because it is important to you. It sounds so trivial, yet it is a profound distinction. It is getting your attention for a reason. If there is a negative emotion involved, then it is usually getting your attention because it is being presented for resolution.

It is interesting to observe what is actually getting and subsequently keeping your attention. Our attention span is limited. In fact, we know that our attention is limited to about 126 bits of information in every second. How do you spend your allotment of attention in each second? Are you directing your attention or is it being directed for you? Are you consciously selecting to focus on those things that increase your well-being and enjoyment of life? If you are not consciously selecting what to focus on, then your programming and surroundings will select it for you. In the case of your programming, things will be brought into your awareness according to a past representation of reality. If you find yourself consistently experiencing negative emotions or looking for what's wrong, then you are being given a chance to resolve those issues by bringing them into your conscious awareness. Failure to resolve them will have the issues return to your unconscious awareness where they will sit until they can surface again at a later time.

> *"Nature never repeats herself, and the possibilities of one human soul will never be found in another."*
>
> – Elizabeth Cady Stanton

Your surroundings can also dictate your attention. If you are easily distracted, then your surroundings will constantly knock your attention off center. In either case, it is still very useful feedback. Where you find your attention focused when you are not deliberately setting it is a clue as to where you are at right now. These clues will lead you to a more powerful state of Being.

FEEDING IT BACK INTO THE SYSTEM

Remember that results in life are pretty black and white. You either get the result that you want or you do not. There is no middle ground. You might have some fantastic reasons for not getting the result that you wanted to get or you might have some really legitimate excuses. But the reality is that you either get it or you don't. My very good friend, and speaker extraordinaire, Bruce Sellery has a great saying that I'd like to borrow to make this point:

No results + a great excuse = NO RESULTS

It doesn't matter why you didn't get a result. I'm not interested in the reasons even though they may be legitimate. If there are reasons, then that means that there aren't any results. Results are not a point of character judgment or worth. Results are results. They are objective. They are not personal. Results are very powerful feedback points as to where you are at, or, more correctly, where you have recently been. Your results are the end result of a feedback loop that started way back with the way you were Being, or your state as we have called it. Remember this state of Being is comprised of mental, emotional and physical components that are all intertwined together. Your response to your internal representation is what really dictated your behaviors, which are what ultimately bring you to your results or lack thereof. Therefore, the results give you feedback on what state of Being brought them about. Your results contain *information* that you can use to live a more powerful and fulfilled life. You have to train yourself how to interpret them so you can glean the learnings easily, effortlessly and consistently.

REAL WANTING

The reason why most people get upset when they don't get what they want goes all the way back to the backwards paradigm of HAVE–DO–BE. Most people expect their results to bring with them a more powerful state of Being than the one they are currently in. But, as we've shown, the paradigm is actually BE–DO–HAVE, so results have nothing to do with your state of Being. Results are the end of the cycle. In the situation where your results match your intended outcomes, then you begin a new cycle. In the situation where your results do not match your intended outcome, then you feed the learnings back into the cycle and have another kick at the can.

The lack of intended results offers a great deal of information. It highlights the *exact* state of Being that is missing. The lack of results illuminates exactly what change you need to make in your state of Being. It all comes by examining how you were trying to use the backwards paradigm to get what you wanted. Remember, in the backwards paradigm your mind erroneously believes that when you finally get something, then you can ultimately achieve a different state of Being (i.e., money will make me happy). Using the understanding that we tend to operate in the backwards paradigm can help us unravel the real wanting underneath our results.

The first thing that you need to do when you have a result that you do not want (i.e., a failure, a crisis, a challenge) is to ask yourself, "Why?" Why do you want that thing? Why do you want the circumstances to be different than what they are? What are you hoping will change if the results change?

Let's look at an example. I was working with a woman named Peggy in a big group seminar that I was doing. I asked her to take an example from her life—something that she wanted that she didn't get. She said that she wanted to have a tropical vacation. When I asked her why she wanted that, she said that she wanted a vacation so she could stop being so stressed at work. I asked her why it was important to her to stop being stressed at work. Her answer indicated that she just wanted some down time to relax. I continued to probe deeper each time asking her why. This went on for a few minutes as she worked through her mind and her model of the world. Finally, she turned to me and said that she really wanted to have this vacation so that she could *be happy*. In her mind she had linked the *having* of a vacation to *being* happy. In her mind, she had decided that she needed this vacation in order to be happy.

Her desire to be happy is her real wanting. This is what she really wants in the moment. Yes, the vacation might be nice, but what she learned is that she really wants to be happy. The fact that she didn't have this vacation served to highlight for her that she wasn't happy in that moment. It served to highlight that she wanted to be happy in that moment. It served to highlight that she had made a choice to give up her power to choose happiness in any moment regardless of the circumstances. The lack of that vacation showed her exactly what she wanted when she wanted it. All that was left to do was to generate a new state of Being that matched the real wanting. In this case, she had the opportunity to choose whether or not she would be happy in the moment versus waiting for something to bring it to her.

THE PHYSICAL REALITY

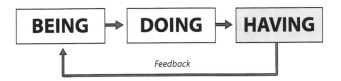

Our results are the end of the energetic cycle. A potential result starts out as exactly that—a potential reality. It does not start out in physical form. It starts out as something invisible; as an idea, as a possibility. In fact, everything that has ever come to be real in our world had its genesis as an idea in the mind of someone. Before the plane could fly, it first had to be thought of in the minds of the Wright brothers. Before the Eiffel Tower was built, it was just a picture in the imagination of Gustav Eiffel. In fact, we often refer to people who achieve great results as "visionaries." We do this because you must first be able to visualize great things before you can achieve great things.

However, great thinking or positive thinking is not enough. An idea gets its power when it is coupled with emotion and a full range of descriptions including sights, sounds, smells and tastes. An idea comes to life when it becomes an internal representation of reality. The more vibrant this internal representation, the more likely the result will come to match it. This idea, when developed into an internal representation, becomes a state of Being. This is when it really becomes a potential reality.

In going from the stage of potential reality to physical reality there is a series of steps that bring the idea into fulfillment. This middle part of the process is called the temporary reality. The idea is beginning to manifest in reality, but it is incomplete. Many steps must be taken to bring it all the way to the final stage. This is the realm of action, maneuvering, building. This part of the cycle is temporary because it does not last forever, nor is it the final result. The end of the cycle is marked by the answer to one question: did you get what you wanted to get or not?

In the classic children's book, *Charlie and the Chocolate Factory* by Roald Dahl, there is a wonderful machine that Willy Wonka has invented to send chocolate via television. First, the idea of sending the chocolate bar originates at the studio. Then, the bar is sent whizzing through the air in a gazillion little pieces where it ultimately rebuilds itself in the TV set at the home of the recipient. Our temporary reality is like the part where the chocolate bar is whizzing through the air. It is an essential part of the process, but it really is the bridge between the idea and the final result.

The physical reality is where you have the outcome of your efforts. Did you produce the outcome that you had intended when it was just an idea—a potential reality? Results are completely objective; either you got it or not. There is no ambiguity. The great news is that every result comes with *more information* or feedback as to what did or didn't work in the process. Your job is to learn how to interpret these results so that you can live an amazing life. A lack of results indicates a lack of congruency in your state of Being. I'll give you a little tip that I've learned over the years. If you are someone who is consciously setting your goals and generally maintaining a positive mindset, then a lack of results *usually* means that your feelings are not in alignment with your conscious thinking. The power lies in ensuring that your emotions are positive and congruent with your thoughts. The physical reality is the end of the cycle. When you use the inherent feedback and go back to the very beginning of the cycle, you are leveraging all the power that you have to create a new and improved result. By the way, the cycle never ends. The Feedback Loop of Life isn't something that you master once and then kick back while life rolls smoothly by. The Feedback Loop of Life describes how the cycle of manifestation works. Your job is to master the cycle so you can live the life you were born to live.

"Our greatest glory is not in never failing,
but in rising every time we fall."
– Confucius

COMPANION ONLINE RESOURCE		**THINK AGAIN!** Visit www.GinaML.com/Chapters to get a summarized version of this chapter for your quick reference.

CHAPTER SIX

THINGS THAT HELP

"Whatever the mind can conceive
and believe, it can achieve."
– Napoleon Hill

There are a number of ways to ensure that you are Being the most powerful version of yourself that you can be. We are always striving for peak performance states or peak experiences whereby the enjoyment of our lives is maximized. Dr. Csikszentmihalyi called these experiences *"flow experiences."* [10] During a flow experience we seem to be in harmony with life and there is little or no resistance. It also seems to be a place where our attention is chiefly focused on what we are doing with very little input from our mind chatter. These experiences lead to highly enjoyable results. There are some strategies that you can use for deliberately creating peak performance states for yourself.

Who you are Being in any given moment is determined by three components that are all interconnected: mental, emotional and physical. Strategies that enhance your state of Being tend to optimize one or more of the three components. Due

---

10   Csikszentmihalyi, Mihaly. *Flow: The Psychology of Optimal Experience*. Harper Perennial Modern Classics, 2008.

to the fact that these three components are inextricably linked, it follows that if you optimize one component, then the other two will follow suit.

HANDLES

Those of you who are scientifically inclined will remember Newton's First Law of Motion, which states that "an object at rest tends to stay at rest and an object in motion tends to stay in motion with the same speed and in the same direction unless acted upon by an unbalanced force." This principle can be applied to human beings as well. Simply put, if we are maintaining a low energy level, we will continue to do so until "acted upon by an unbalanced force," which means we must change our state of Being.

When you are low, it is common to feel as though you are spiraling downwards and that things are getting worse and worse. Don't fret; this is simply a function of your focus, which is part of the mental component of your state. Focusing on what is wrong will always bring about more of what is wrong. It seems like a vicious cycle with no apparent way out. The most powerful way to change your state is to choose a different focus. This isn't always easy to do, especially when you feel as though you are plummeting.

A powerful analogy to help you shift out of this downward spiral is to think of grabbing onto a handle. As you grab the handle, your decline halts immediately. At this point, you are free to use the handle to begin your climb back up to a higher state of Being. I use the term "handles" to describe techniques that you can use to instantly halt a decline as you feel it happening. You don't need to use every handle in every situation. However, you must make the choice to use what help is readily available to you. The handle will not grab you; you must choose to grab it. As always, the choice and the responsibility are yours. I will describe some powerful handles, beginning with the simple act of breathing.

BREATHING (physical)

Oxygen is the most important nutrient for our bodies. Consider that we can last weeks without food, days without water, but we cannot withstand but a few minutes without oxygen. Most systems and organs in the body require oxygen to function at their optimal levels. In 1931, Dr. Otto Warburg was awarded the Nobel Prize in Medicine for his discovery of the link between cells, oxygen and cancer. He described his discovery during a famous speech to Nobel Laureates in 1966 when he said, "Cancer, above all other diseases, has countless secondary causes. Almost anything can cause cancer. But, even for cancer, there is only one prime cause. The prime cause of cancer is the replacement of the respiration of oxygen (oxidation of sugar) in normal body cells by fermentation of sugar." [11] Every time Otto Warburg lowered the oxygen level by 35 percent in a healthy cell, it became cancerous. In other words, cancer is not compatible with a healthy pH environment full of oxygen.

Heart disease also has a link to oxygen. The work done

---

11   Warburg, Otto. "The Prime Cause and Prevention of Cancer—a lecture delivered to Nobel Laureates at Lindau, Lake Constance, Germany." June 30, 1966.

at Baylor University in Texas has shown that one can reverse arterial disease in monkeys by infusing oxygen into the diseased arteries. When the heart is deprived of oxygen due to a blockage in circulation, the result is a heart attack. When this happens in the brain, the result is a stroke. It makes sense then that we should aim to increase the supply of oxygen to our bodies. Breathing is our main mechanism for doing this.

The breath and breathing techniques have been studied for thousands of years. And for good reason. Breathing is the fastest way to change your state of Being. The physiological aspects of breathing have been extensively studied including things like the levels of oxygen, nitrogen and carbon dioxide. These elements play a role in how effective the breath is in the processes of the body. Breathing has also been studied for its role as a bridge between the body and the soul. Many

> *"He lives most life who breathes most air."*
>
> – Elizabeth Barrett Browning

ancient traditions ascertained that focusing on the breath allows you to quiet your mind chatter and connect to your inner self. Doing so increases your awareness of who you really are. Suffice it to say that breathing is a very important function and one that often goes unnoticed. There are two important factors to look at for optimal performance. These include both your breathing technique and your breathing frequency.

One of the first things that happens when a person is in a stressful situation is a change in breathing. In these stressful moments, the mind is usually engaged in a stress response and generating thoughts that are negative. As we know from earlier chapters, the key in any stressful situation is to gain control of your response such that it is appropriate to the situation at hand. If a stress response is unwarranted, then you have the power to override the response. The key to getting access to your common sense is to calm down. One of the best ways to calm yourself down is slow, rhythmic diaphragmatic breathing. Once you have shifted away from a stress response, then your brain will be able to receive more organized input from your body, allowing you to think better and be more creative.

The proper way to breathe is to breathe diaphragmatically. This is also called abdominal breathing. If you've ever watched a baby breathe then you have seen diaphragmatic breathing. The baby's belly rises on the inhalation and falls on the exhalation. In diaphragmatic breathing, the abdominal muscles expand and contract when we breathe instead of the chest muscles. The diaphragm is a small muscle attached to the bottom of the lungs. When the abdominal muscles expand upon inhalation, the diaphragm pulls the lungs down, elongating them. Likewise, when the abdominal muscles contract upon exhalation, the diaphragm allows the lungs to move upwards and expel air. When the abdominal muscles are used for breathing instead of the chest muscles, then a message is sent to the heart and lungs to slow down and relax. This allows for optimal physiological and psychological performance. An optimal breathing rate is considered to be five to six breaths per minute.

You can try this for yourself. Make sure you are sitting up straight and comfortable with your legs uncrossed. Put one hand on your chest and one hand on your belly. Remember, you want your chest to remain still so you shouldn't feel any movement on the hand on your chest. Start by taking an inhalation through your nose and allowing your abdominal muscles to expand and your belly to rise. Then, contract your abdominal muscles and push your belly in and push the air out of the your lungs. Do this to a count of five. Count 1, 2, 3 ,4, 5 on the inhalation and then 1, 2, 3, 4, 5 on the exhalation. Each count should last about one second. Doing this for just one minute will send a message to your heart and lungs to calm down, thus arresting any stress response. Doing this for 10 minutes will allow your body to begin to produce the desired hormones and biochemicals necessary for your well-being. When you are in this state of well-being, you will be able to access all of your creativity and problem-solving skills. You will be aware of more choices in your situations and be able to respond with grace and ease.

Another amazing thing that happens when you focus on breathing diaphragmatically (and with intention), is that you are said to increase your physiological coherence. Physiological coherence is a term that is used to describe the harmony in your body's systems. Breathing properly with intention allows you to calm your emotions and tune into what is needed in the moment, thus allowing you to choose a positive emotion over a preprogrammed reactionary negative one. Researchers at the Institute of HeartMath have shown that positive emotions actually increase the synchronization of the body's systems. This leads to more increased energy, efficiency and effectiveness. There is a link between the emotions and the physiological well-being of a person. The breath is a gateway to coherence because it allows you to calm the mind and the body thus increasing the choices available to you in any situation.

POSTURE (physical)

The position of your body plays a role in your state of Being. Small receptors throughout your body are always sending signals to your brain as to which state you are in. If your posture is strong, confident and free of restriction then your brain will respond accordingly. Likewise if your posture is shrunken, hunched and defeated, then that is the message that will go to your brain. There are many physiological benefits to good posture. Good posture makes it easier to breathe properly. It also improves circulation and digestion by minimizing restrictions. Finally, good posture helps your joints, muscles and your spine by keeping you in proper alignment, again allowing things to flow in your body without restrictions.

> "Smiling is very important. If we are not able to smile, then the world will not have peace. It is not by going out for a demonstration against nuclear missiles that we can bring about peace. It is with our capacity of smiling, breathing and being peace that we can make peace."
>
> – Thich Nhat Hanh

Changing your posture is a quick way to change your state of Being, particularly if you find yourself in a negative state. If you simply assume the posture of your desired state, you will find it easier to actually achieve that state of Being. Think about what happens when you jump into action after lying around on the couch. Your change in posture initiates changes in your body to allow you to change your state of Being.

Let's get you into a peak performance state right now. A peak performance posture is one where you body is elongated. Imagine a string pulling the top of your head towards the sky. Stand up now and put yourself in this position. Ensure that your feet are firmly planted on the ground about shoulder-width apart. This stance should feel very centered and powerful. Your shoulders should be relaxed and down and your eyes focused ahead. You can teach yourself to connect this peak performance posture to a peak state of Being through the anchoring techniques that we covered in chapter three. Soon enough, you will find that you are able to instantly shift into your peak state of Being simply by shifting into the posture that accompanies it.

Another obvious shift in posture is through movement. Movement of your body is a very effective way of shifting your state of Being. Movement includes things such as exercise, dancing, walking, running and jumping. Basically, any time you change the way your body is moving, you automatically change your emotional and mental states. This is especially true if you have been stuck in a certain state of Being that is negative and not producing the results that you want. Movement causes your energy to change. This change causes a whole host of things to change including your physiology, your mental and emotional states and your focus. Often times, the best thing you can do when you are stuck on a problem is to leave the problem and do something active. This will serve to clear your head and allow you to take a fresh perspective on the problem when you return. Usually, the movement break has allowed you to access alternatives that were not previously available.

NOURISHMENT (physical)

Another important way to keep yourself in a peak performance state is to fuel your body with food that serves this purpose. There is a definite correlation between food and your energy levels as well as the state of your mind. What you put in your body has a profound effect on your energy levels. You may have heard the adage, "Garbage in, garbage out." We must be mindful of what we're putting into our bodies because the functionality of our physical bodies is extremely important.

> *"Inward calm cannot be maintained unless physical strength is constantly and intelligently replenished."*
> *– Buddha*

I don't need to tell you what happens if your body ceases to function. Food is the body's fuel. Think of your body as a high-performance automobile. When you buy a high-end car, the manufacturer insists you use only premium-grade gasoline because the engine will not function at insufficient levels of octane. This is the same for the human body. If you continuously use low-grade fuel, your performance will be adversely affected.

The better the fuel you put into your body, the better performance you can expect. It is much easier to transform high-quality fuel into high-quality energy. You must focus your efforts on using fuel that serves to increase and maintain your energy levels instead of fuels that provide a quick burst of energy followed by a sharp decline. Your best bet is to eat a diet that is as natural as possible with a minimal amount of processing, pesticides and modifications. Increasing the amount of organic food in your diet not only gives you a better source of nutrients, but it also encourages farming practices that reduce the burden placed on the earth.

There have been a number of foods identified as "superfoods" because they do so much good for the body that we should go out of our way to get them. It is important to remember that there is not one perfect food but rather a variety of foods that give your body what it needs. *The New York Times* ran an article in 2008 listing the 11 best foods that delivered benefits such as nutrients, vitamins, minerals, enzymes, antioxidants, along with many others. The article was based on the research of Nutritionist and author Dr. Jonny Bowden. Below is a list of foods from *The New York Times* article combined with some of the favorites from Dr. Bowden's book called *The 150 Healthiest Foods on Earth*.[12] Try to incorporate some of these foods into your diet to help keep your body running in peak state.

- Any dark green leafy vegetable (swiss chard, spinach, arugula, purslane, etc.)
- Blueberries
- Beets

---

12   Bowden, Johnny. *The 150 Healthiest Foods on Earth: The Surprising, Unbiased Truth About What You Should Eat and Why.* Fair Winds Press, 2007.

- Cabbage
- Cinnamon
- Mangosteen
- Pomegranate Juice
- Dried plums (aka prunes)
- Pumpkin Seeds
- Sardines
- Tumeric
- Pumpkin
- Goji berries
- Salmon
- Quinoa
- Artichokes

GRATITUDE (emotional)

Gratitude has the power to immediately reverse any negative energy. When we shift into gratitude, we have literally flipped an energetic switch. Given that gratitude only resides in the present moment, we will feel an instant shift in our energy level. Consider that you cannot be grateful and hateful at the same time.

> "Gratitude is not only the greatest of virtues, but the parent of all the others."
>
> – Cicero

Studies have shown that an attitude of gratitude actually affects the physical world immediately, and this includes the human body. Dr. Masaru Emoto is famous for his "Hidden Messages in Water" experiments that have shown the effect of gratitude on water molecules in the form of ice crystals. When placed in the presence of loving and grateful energy, Emoto found that the crystals organized themselves into beautiful patterns. Conversely, when placed in the presence of hateful and negative energy, the crystals arranged themselves erratically with chaos and disharmony dominating.[13] Consider that the human body is approximately 70 percent water and you will quickly realize the powerful effect that positive emotions can have on your health.

Practicing gratitude is a very active state of creation. This is not something that just happens; it takes intention to be grateful. When we focus our intention on gratitude, all negative energy falls away and we are instantly filled with powerful, loving, positive energy. Gratitude is also remarkable in its pure simplicity. All that is required is the intention to be grateful in the present moment. That's it; nothing more. Simply be thankful for what is, exactly as it is, exactly right now. What could be easier? The only thing you must do to use this handle is to look around, find things to be grateful for and feel gratitude flood your heart in the present moment.

You don't need to be creative about it or elaborate, complicated or sophisticated. You simply look at your present circumstances and choose the one thing that is irritating you the most. This heightened irritation is a signal that this situation is calling for resolution. You want to choose it and heal it instantly with gratitude. So, take the one thing that is most irritating or upsetting to you now and, in this moment, choose to feel grateful for

---

13   Emoto, Masaru. Translated by David A. Thayne. *The Hidden Messages in Water*. Hillsboro, OR: Beyond Words Publishing Inc., 2004.

it. Approach the situation as if there is something to be grateful for. If you search for the learning long enough, it will eventually emerge. The moment you find true gratitude, the irritation will be released and in its place will be unconditional love.

My husband and I have a technique for instantly shifting our energy. When one of us is irritated with the other, that person is charged with the task of finding gratitude immediately. This has never failed to instantly dissolve the dispute. The hardest part, of course, is choosing to be grateful in a moment of irritation. But once the commitment to gratitude is made, the irritation disappears.

THE GRATITUDE HANDLE

Pick a situation in your life that gives you trouble and write it down here: _____

_____

_____

Now, take two minutes to brainstorm things to be grateful for in that situation. The trick to this exercise it to do it quickly. Don't judge your responses. Take the time to really focus on something to be grateful for. You will be surprised at what you discover. _____

_____

_____

_____

_____

_____

_____

Using gratitude is not a new technique. In fact, it is one of the most ancient secrets in humanity. All great spiritual leaders have taught the practice of gratitude in one form or another. I remember reading an article about an interview with the Dalai Lama that astounded me. When asked what the Dalai Lama thought of China, his response was simply "gratitude." Imagine how our lives could change if we replaced all negative emotions with the positive, loving energy of gratitude. We just might find peace and happiness in the most unlikely place: within ourselves. Imagine how this shift in each of us might affect the world!

FORGIVENESS (emotional)

When we hold a grudge against another person, we are emotionally bound to that person. It takes a great deal of energy to maintain a grudge. More often than not, the other person does not even realize we are holding negative energy against her or him. It's possible that the other person is not spending any energy at all. But we certainly are.

Forgiveness is not really an emotion. It is more accurately described as a decision that we make to *release* negative emotions. The word "forgiveness" comes from the old English *gi-fan*, which means "to give." Combined with the prefix "for" as in forward, the word forgiveness means *to give forward*. We are forgiving the limiting aspects of who we are and reclaiming a part of ourselves. In Jung's definition of the "shadow aspect," we project

> "To forgive is to set a prisoner free and discover the prisoner was YOU."
>
> – Author unknown

these limiting aspects onto others, thereby disowning them. In this context, all forgiveness is self-forgiveness as you reclaim the projected aspects of yourself. Through forgiveness you are giving a sense of acceptance to yourself going forward—you are reclaiming your whole self as you evolve and grow.

If you look into your "mirror of life" and see a perceived wrongdoing, you must remember that you need to change on the inside before you will see a different reflection on the outside. Forgiveness gives you access to your inner world and allows you to shift who you are Being. The reflection on the outside will change instantaneously. The situation will no longer have any power over you.

If you find that you are simply unable to forgive someone for something she or he has done to you, consider that you have not yet healed the wound that the person has brought to your attention. The act of forgiveness is a release, which means that you must also be willing to release the pain you are feeling as a result of the situation. The act of forgiveness gives us the ability to heal the wound and release the negativity surrounding it. An amazing paradox about forgiveness is that when we have truly forgiven a person, we actually become grateful to her or him for providing us with such an accurate reflection of what needed to be healed inside us. Forgiveness is one of the most powerful choices we can make.

MUSIC (emotional)

Several studies have shown that certain types of music have a very positive effect on the body. Specifically, classical music influences positive emotions and helps to counterbalance the effects of stress so prevalent in modern life. Dr. Charles Kimble from Dayton University has discovered that people can change a bad mood into a good one simply by listening to classical music.[14]

Music therapy is being used in the treatment of all sorts of ailments, even cancer. Music has been shown to lower blood pressure, normalize heart rates and increase the production of endorphins in the brain. All of these lead to an overall increased level of relaxation, which feels good. Remember that feeling good is a key to maintaining a positive state of Being. Music is a way to direct your feelings such that you can marry them with the thoughts about what it is you want in life.

The type of music does make a difference in creating these feelings in the body. Classical music seems to be the most effective at creating strong positive emotions. The main indicator, though, is how you feel in response to the music. If you feel uplifted and positive when listening to any beautiful music, you should keep this music available for times when you need a boost. Using music to enhance your mood is a quick way to access good feelings so you can attach them to your thoughts of what you want.

MEDITATION (mental)

Meditation is a practice whereby one moves beyond reactive thinking into a deeper state of awareness. The word meditation originally comes from the Indo-European word "med" meaning "to measure." It entered English from two Latin words: *meditari* (to think, to dwell upon, to exercise the mind) and *mederi* (to heal). Its Sanskrit derivation *medha* means wisdom.

---

14   As cited by Marcus Wynne, "Emotions in Motion," *Psychology Today.* Nov-Dec 1998. www.psychologytoday.com.

Simply put, meditation is the self-regulation of your awareness for your well-being.

Meditation is a technique for resting the mind so that it can rejuvenate. It is not to be confused with sleeping or day-dreaming. When you meditate you are completely awake and alert. The difference is that you are focused inward instead of outward. Most of us have never been trained to focus inward and the process of meditating is challenging and frustrating. This is because it is quite difficult to quiet the mind chatter. Until we begin

> "Meditation brings wisdom; lack of meditation leaves ignorance. Know well what leads you forward and what holds you back, and choose the path that leads to wisdom."
>
> – Buddha

to meditate, we don't appreciate just how active our mind chatter is. Think of how much of your attention is spent on your internal dialogue. Mind chatter is the culmination of all of your descriptions, explanations and models of your reality, and the chatter usually runs nonstop while you are awake. In order to get in touch with all that is really possible in your reality, you have to learn to quiet your mind. Meditation can produce profound results.

Consider that when a group of over 4,000 people from 62 countries gathered to practice a series of Transcendental Meditations in the city of Washington, D.C., in July 1993, the violent crime rate dropped 21 percent on that day.[15] What is

---

15   Hagelin, et al, *Effects of Group Practice of the Transcendental Meditation Program on Preventing Violent Crime in Washington, DC: Results of the National Demonstration Project, June–July 1993.* (Fairfield, Iowa: Institute of Science, Technology and Public Policy, Maharishi University of Management, 1993).

even more astounding is that the group predicted the crime rate drop because they had been producing similar results elsewhere. Imagine what would happen if the collective consciousness (all of us as a group) focused its intentions on love and unity instead of war and separation. There are six billion people on this planet, and my guess is we could affect a massive change with very little effort.

There are many different forms of meditation. It is not necessarily a religious practice, but because of its inherent spiritual aspects it is integral to many religions. Meditation can be practiced through concentration, mindfulness, yoga and prayer. It is also possible to meditate or quiet the mind through physical movement. This is sometimes called "active meditation" because the body is in motion. While the forms of meditation greatly vary, the purpose is always the same: to quiet the mind and observe what is happening. The idea is that when the mind is calm, we can be present to the peace and calm that is all around us.

How you meditate is not as important as *whether* you meditate. You would be well served to find a meditative technique that works for you. Remember that the difference between your model of reality and what is actually happening or available is the mind chatter or description of what is happening. If you quiet your mind chatter, then your model of reality can better represent all of the possibilities that are available to you. This is what it means to have an open mind in that you are open to seeing the multitude of possibilities that are available right in front of you.

AFFIRMATIONS (mental)

Language is one of the most powerful tools human beings have that differentiates us from other creatures. Our spoken words can have powerful effects on our energy levels. We must choose our language to correspond with the energy level we are trying to achieve. Simply choosing to alter our language will have an instant effect on our energy levels. Consider the example of the following two sentences, both reflecting the same situation:

"This hike is killing me."

"This hike is challenging me."

Each statement will have a profoundly different effect on the body. In the first instance, the body will respond to the negative energy with a similarly low energetic response, such that the person hiking will find that the hike continues to be a struggle. The second sentence will likely inspire the body to increase its energy level to meet the challenge of the situation. Positive language empowers and inspires a desire to improve.

Declaring our intentions in a positive way is a key step to realizing them. Another important guideline for affirmations is that they must be made in the present tense. If we declare our intention in the future tense, it will always remain in the future, never coming to fruition. Another important aspect of affirmations is that they must go beyond words and thought and include emotions as well. In fact, the affirmation should include as much of the internal representation as possible including components that correlate to the five senses. In this way, an affirmation becomes a potential reality; a possible version of your reality that has yet to come to fruition.

Visualization is a technique that has been used extensively in the field of competitive sports. Elite athletes are taught to visualize their desired performance with as much vivid detail as if it were really happening. The results of this technique are astounding. Studies using body monitors have shown that the same muscles fire in the same sequence and at the same time during the visualization as in the real competition. The mind is unable to distinguish the real performance from the visualized performance. In this way, the visualization serves as a virtual training reality in which the athlete can perfect the skills required for peak performance. By combining your declared intention with your ability to visualize and construct a "virtual reality," you will create a very powerful affirmation that includes all aspects of experience.

The power of this technique will increase as you are able to engage all your senses in your affirmation. You need to make the effort to provide as much detail as possible when experiencing your affirmation, including the sights, smells, sounds, tastes, feelings and positive thoughts that are present. Then, you must repeat your affirmation as often as possible throughout the day to reinforce the feelings and positive energy. A great technique for shifting out of a downward spiral of self-doubt is to visualize your end result in terms of the impact it will have on

> *"Live with intention. Walk to the edge. Listen hard. Practice wellness. Play with abandon. Laugh. Choose with no regret. Appreciate your friends. Continue to learn. Do what you love. Live as if this is all there is."*
>
> – Mary Anne Radmacher

others' lives. Shifting the benefit and focus away from yourself and on to other human beings is usually sufficient to shift your negative energy in the present back to a higher level.

TAKING THE "im" OUT OF imPOSSIBLE (mental)

The mind tends to divide the world into 1) things that are possible and 2) things that are impossible. If we conform to these constraints, we are limiting ourselves on what we can achieve. If you are feeling particularly stuck, a great way to get moving is to pick something that is im*possible* to do and then do it. Once you have achieved the im*possible*, you are free to explore what other things might also be possible. Taking the "im" out of im*possible* allows you to dissolve the dividing line between what is possible and what is not. Once this line has been eliminated, you have the opportunity to reclassify anything that seems impossible.

I developed this technique at a time in my life when I was feeling quite stuck in my own limits. I was a new mother faced with trying to do everything right while being incredibly sleep deprived. I had always been used to doing things efficiently, effortlessly and with a great deal of success. New motherhood was a big challenge for me because I had never done it before and was left feeling inadequate most of the time. Things were quite low for me and I didn't know what else to do. I had to catapult myself out of the state that I was in. Out of my despair came a very useful tool.

Being good at motherhood was sitting firmly in my "impossible" category. I decided to randomly pick something else from my im*possible* category and take on the challenge of achieving it. My thinking was that if I could achieve something else in my im*possible* category then perhaps I could reclassify motherhood.

I chose running a marathon. Finishing a marathon might not seem like much to most

> "People who say it cannot be done should not interrupt those who are doing it."
>
> – George Bernard Shaw

people, but believe me when I tell you that I am not a marathoner and it was probably more likely that pigs would fly. However, I took it on. I became a marathoner in the moment that I decided to do it. I filled my days with training and visualizations.

The race provided me with one of those insightful, life-changing moments where things are never the same again. I hit "the wall" at Mile 17 of the Nike Women's Marathon in San Francisco. I was fine at the bottom of this giant hill, but by the time I reached the top I was finished. My body shut down. My mind shut down. I was in complete despair. Then, my husband, who happened to be on the sidelines at Mile 17, asked one mundane question about some of the people that had supported my race and my fundraising efforts and along came another cosmic two by four. In an instant, I finally understood what it meant to be the source of my own angst and that a shift in my own beliefs and Being was all that was needed to overcome even the most insurmountable obstacles. I was the only one who didn't believe in me. I changed this thought and my entire reality changed immediately. My ego dissolved the instant I realized that finishing that race came down to one choice I had to make about myself. In choosing to shift my belief about myself, I was able to overcome all the physical challenges that had doomed my race minutes earlier. They literally vanished. At the moment I crossed that finish line, I knew I had shifted to a completely different level. You are reading this book because I finished that race.

Take what is im*possible* for you and do it. Then start knocking off all the other things that used to be im*possible* and aren't anymore. Once you deconstruct the division between im*possible* and *possible*, you will have shifted to a new state of Being, never to return again.

FAITH (mental/emotional)

The definition of faith is "a belief that is not based on proof." Cultivating faith is a skill that will serve you well. Nobody knows for sure how this Universe of ours works. We all have our theories but at the end of the day, there is no proof. Faith is important because it allows you to believe in something bigger than you. It allows you to trust that everything is as it should be. Faith is what you can turn to when you seem to be out of options.

> "Faith is an oasis in the heart which can never be reached by the caravan of thinking."
> – Kahlil Gibran

Instead of desperately trying to control your circumstances, it would be better to learn to control your responses. When these responses are grounded in faith, you will feel stronger and more certain that you are on the right path for growth. Having faith makes it less likely that a negative event in your life will completely throw you out of a peak state. Having faith means that you will be grounded on the inside so that circumstances on the outside will have less effect on your overall state of Being.

They call it a "leap of faith" because at some point we must surrender the mind's need to have proof that it will work. At some point we must trust in the inner knowing that exists deep within us. At some point we must give in to the possibility that anything might be possible and recognize that the only thing we can change is ourselves. At some point we must accept responsibility for our choices and reclaim the power that is already within us: the power to choose, the power to change and the power to create a reality that is absolutely perfect for us. Heaven is not a place to get to in the future; heaven is right here, right now. We need only see what is right in front of us. It all depends on what you focus on. Out of the millions of available bits of information in each second, which 126 do you set your mind on?

I had the opportunity to meet an amazing woman named Elizabeth. When Elizabeth was about 50 years old, she was taken to the hospital with suspected appendicitis. When they opened her up, they discovered a huge tumor instead. Her appendix was fine, but she was diagnosed with bowel cancer and given weeks to live. The nurses and doctors expected her to freak out, but she didn't do that. She told me that she didn't see the point in freaking out because it wouldn't have changed anything. The doctors told her that they could do a surgery that *might* get the tumor, but it was risky and required blood transfusions. This violated Elizabeth's beliefs, so she sought a Naturopath instead in an effort to address her situation. She told me that she did exactly as she was told by her Naturopath. She also prayed a lot. But she didn't pray for what you would expect. She didn't pray for the tumor to disappear; she didn't pray for alternative circumstances at all. She prayed to be given the strength to deal with whatever came her way. She turned to her family and friends for support and continued to pray for strength. She told me that she never got angry for having these circumstances because she had faith that this was a meaningful part of her life experience, come what may. She took it one day at a time, never expecting anything other than what it was. Within days, she felt better although she tells me that it took about five years before she was completely well again. The miraculous part of this story is that she continues to thrive more than 25 years after they told her she only had weeks to live.

I believe that there were a number of things that contributed to Elizabeth's recovery. First of all, she maintained complete control of her response to her situation. Grounded in her faith that her circumstances were a meaningful part of her life experience, she was able to accept the news of her tumor without any negative emotions. Secondly, she called upon her faith through her prayers. But, instead of asking for a change in circumstances, she asked instead for strength. This allowed her to look for sources of strength instead of focusing her attention on her disease. In fact, the disease got none of her conscious attention. Finally, she surrounded herself with people that supported her healing journey and who believed that anything was possible. This helped her to reinforce the belief within herself. The results were many, many more years to enjoy loved ones, such as her grandchildren, and even to help others who faced the same problems. When I asked her if she would have changed a thing, her reply was a firm "no."

"Sometimes your only available
transportation is a leap of faith."
– Margaret Shepherd

COMPANION ONLINE RESOURCE	THINK AGAIN!
	Visit www.GinaML.com/Chapters to get a summarized version of this chapter for your quick reference.

CHAPTER SEVEN

~~~~~~~~~~

THINGS THAT DON'T

"We all cling to the past and because we cling to the past,
we become unavailable to the present."
– *Bhagwan Shree Rajneesh (Osho)*

As opposed to the previous chapter, this chapter outlines a few pitfalls to avoid along the path of life. The things that don't help all fall into the category of "energy-suckers." None of the things described in this chapter support our growth or help us maintain a peak performance state. We need to be aware of the effects of these energy-suckers so that we can recognize and avoid them when we encounter them. Be forewarned that if we spend any amount of our hard-earned energy thinking about these energy-suckers, we will actually empower them. It is best to steer clear of them altogether, without so much as a passing glance.

Remember that what you focus on expands. Even if you focus on NOT wanting to indulge in any of these energy-suckers, you are still giving them your energy and they will continue to be present. If you experience any of these energy-suckers, just turn in the opposite direction or, better yet, employ one of the strategies from the previous chapter for shifting your focus.

IMPROPER BREATHING TECHNIQUES (physical)

Restricted breathing techniques can lead to ill health and a lack of well-being due to insufficient levels of oxygen that are needed for optimal function. The issue with poor breathing is that usually it is a habit that has been formed over many years of repetition. It goes mainly unnoticed and is usually the result of a habitual stress response even if the situation doesn't warrant a stress response. The three most prevalent improper breathing techniques include chronic hyperventilation, chest breathing and reverse breathing.

It has been said that most people today are chronic hyperventilators. The issue with hyperventilation is not a lack of oxygen as one might assume. The issue is the loss of too much carbon dioxide. Carbon dioxide is important in maintaining the pH of the blood. Even the smallest deviations in pH in the body can cause adverse effects in the cells and processes of the body. The body does whatever it needs to do

> "No one can get inner peace by pouncing on it."
> – Harry Emerson Fosdick

to maintain a constant pH. Acute hyperventilation is a state of breathing that is faster or deeper than necessary and can cause undesirable symptoms such as dizziness and headaches. It is usually classified as over 20 breaths per minute. By comparison, chronic hyperventilation doesn't have the obvious causes or symptoms of acute hyperventilation. In chronic hyperventilation, an accelerated breathing rate coupled with the improper techniques of chest breathing indicate to the body that it should initiate a stress response, which of course is unhealthy on a continual basis. Chronic hyperventilation occurs at around 12–15 breaths per minute.

It is interesting to do a baseline test to understand where you are with your breathing rate. Without changing anything, time yourself for one minute breathing in and out. Each full breath including an inhalation and an exhalation counts as "one breath." Once you have determined your breathing rate, then you can start to understand the effects that your breathing has on your well-being.

If you've indentified yourself as someone who consistently breathes more than 12 breaths per minute then consider making it a regular practice to reduce your breathing rate. This is most easily achieved using the diaphragmatic breathing techniques from the previous chapter. An optimal resting breathing rate is 5–6 breaths per minute. The more frequently that you become aware of your breathing rate, the easier it will be to maintain a consistently slower breathing rate.

Our lungs are designed to breathe in two different ways: chest expansion or diaphragmatic breathing. If your chest expands and contracts when you breathe then you are literally initiating a stress response in your body. It has been shown that when you chest breathe the muscles in your chest send messages to your heart and lungs to increase heart rate and inhalation. This is the first step in activating your stress (fight-or-flight) response. The interesting observation is that most of us breathe this way all the time, constantly sending a physiological message to the brain that we are in a stressful situation even when we are not. Over the years, most of us have forgotten the proper way to breathe and have defaulted to chest breathing.

Reverse breathing occurs when the abdomen moves in on the inhalation and out on the exhalation. This is the reverse of the diaphragmatic breathing that we discussed in the previous chapter. Recall that the belly should move out on the inhalation in order to allow the lungs to expand fully downwards. Reverse breathing is a result of many factors including physical constrictions such as tight waistbands as well as social conditioning. I have visions of Popeye sucking in his belly when he took a breath to pump out his chest to impress Olive Oyl. Many people are taught to "suck in their gut" in order to look more appealing. The problem is that when you prevent your lungs from expanding downwards you impede your ability to take in adequate levels of oxygen, not to mention you also place undue stress and tension on muscles that were never intended to be used for daily breathing. This could lead to chronic tension in the neck and shoulder area.

The answer to all of these improper breathing techniques is to practice diaphragmatic breathing. An optimal rate is 5–6 breaths per minute. Begin by practicing this for 5–10 minutes each day and you will find that it becomes easier and easier to give your body the oxygen it needs to keep you in peak performance state.

TOXINS (physical)

Our environment contains numerous toxins. In and of itself, this is not disastrous, as the body is designed to efficiently and effectively process toxins. A problem arises, however, when there is a toxic overload or a breakdown in the body's ability to process toxins. When this occurs, there is a build-up of toxicity that eventually leads to breakdown or disease. There are only two ways to avoid this: 1) reduce your exposure to toxins and/or 2) maintain the efficient performance of the body's natural abilities to eliminate toxins.

Unfortunately, we are currently experiencing a toxic overload in our culture as we continue to poison our air, our water and even our food supply. Our best bet is to avoid as many toxins as possible. Recognize, however, that it is not necessary to completely eliminate all toxins, because the body has an incredible ability to process them. You don't need to feel threatened or angry or to freak out if you are exposed to toxins. This reaction just keeps your energy focused at a low level. Rather, you need to be mindful of the toxins you are exposed to and avoid them as much as possible. Bear in mind that a negative thought and a negative emotion can have more toxic power than most of these physical toxins.

Alkaline pH levels in the bloodstream have been correlated to well-being and health. PH is a measure of acidity or alkalinity of a solution. A neutral pH is defined as 7.0. Anything below 7.0 is considered acidic and anything above 7.0 is considered alkaline. The aforementioned Dr. Otto Warburg through the course of his studies found that cancer is not compatible with a slightly alkaline pH environment full of oxygen.

Healthy cells have a slightly alkaline pH and a high oxygen content whereas cancer cells have an extremely acidic pH and a very short supply of oxygen (if any). Maintaining appropriate alkalinity is important for our health and well-being. Acidic conditions provide favorable conditions for the growth of bacteria, yeast, fungus and other microorganisms. Many health practitioners concur that the maintenance of an alkaline pH is essential for our cellular health. Many of our environmental toxins produce acidic conditions. Over 100,000 new chemicals have been introduced to our foods, air and water. Consider the term "acid rain," which is used to describe unusually acidic precipitation caused by emissions that react in the atmosphere to produce acids. The food that we eat greatly affects our pH. As a general rule, anything that is processed is usually acidic in the body including processed sugars, artificial sweeteners and junk foods. The optimal diet consists of over 80 percent alkaline forming foods with only 20 percent of the diet coming from acid-forming foods.

Food additives and other chemicals that are added to food place a huge burden on the body. They are not natural, so they must be processed by the body. They provide little, if any, nutritional value and serve only to consume the body's energy, thereby reducing its overall effectiveness in processing everything in our systems. We must be

> "Purity and simplicity are the two wings with which man soars above the Earth and all temporary nature."
>
> – Thomas à Kempis

very wary of any foods containing additives, fillers, artificial sweeteners, coloring and flavoring. These compounds add unnecessary stress to our systems, which could lead to the ultimate breakdown in the body's ability to do its job. Again, it is about making choices that keep you in a powerful state of Being. You usually have more control over your food choices than you do over your environmental factors. Being mindful of your food selection is a relatively easy way to help your body and your mind maintain peak states.

Our modern food supply places a great burden on our bodies to handle all the modifications, additives, pesticides and processing that have become commonplace. Studies conducted in Australia and Britain show that the nutrient levels of many vegetables have significantly declined due to the lack of good quality soil as a result of farming practices that do not allow for sufficient time for soil reconstitution. That means that even the foods that we consider to be highly nutritious have suffered from modern farming techniques and practices.

Numerous studies have shown that processed sugar and flour greatly reduce the performance and attention span of children in school. So why do we continue to fuel our children with packaged, processed foods and then wonder why we have an epidemic of attention deficit?

We have several very powerful choices that can keep our toxic overload from food to a minimum. Most mainstream modern farming practices are designed to maximize production levels at the minimum cost. They are not intended to maximize nutrient levels. Pesticide use, genetic modification, hormone injections, antibiotic use and non-sustainable farming practices all lead to an increased level of toxicity in our food supply. Our best bet is to, when possible, avoid food products that were made using these methods. Choosing organic foods decreases our overall exposure to toxins, thus reducing the stress on our systems to process them. It just makes sense to ingest as few toxins as possible.

As with our food supply, our air and water supplies are also bombarded with toxins. These days, air and water pollution are commonplace. Being mindful of how much toxicity you are exposed to is the first step in managing it. If it can get into your body then your body will have to deal with eliminating the toxin. Your body is designed to eliminate toxins efficiently. The issue arises when the toxic load is more than your body can handle. If you live in an area where there is a lot of air and water pollution, you must pay attention to the other sources of toxins in your life. Alternatively, if you live in an area where the air and water are clean and pure, you have a little breathing room when it comes to other toxins. Remember, your goal is to place as little burden as possible on your body's natural system for eliminating toxins.

ALLOWING FEAR TO DOMINATE (emotional)

Fear is a natural emotion created in response to a belief that we are not safe. Everyone has fears. Acknowledging our fears and being controlled by our fears are two totally different things. When we acknowledge our fear, it means we are allowing the energy to pass through as we experience the events of life. When we are controlled by our fear, it means we focus our attention on the fear and the story about the fear, thus empowering the fear energy to control our actions. The mind uses fear as a tool to keep us in our comfort zone. The problem is that fear is one of the lowest vibrating emotions, so we are only going to notice other low vibrations when in a state of fear. This will keep us from focusing on anything in the realm of love, peace or happiness. Allowing your fear to prevail prevents you from receiving what you want.

However, fear can also be a gift because it indicates exactly which parts of us need to be healed in order to remove any blockages in energy. It is important, therefore, not to ignore our fears but rather to learn to use them to help us get what we want. Fear is just a signal from the mind that danger is present.

> "Courage is not the absence of fear, but rather the judgment that something else is more important than fear."
>
> – Ambrose Redmoon

We can use our fear to understand exactly what our minds perceive as dangerous and to determine in the moment if this is true. The issue likely resides in an outdated internal representation or model of Reality. Usually most fears are created in childhood and no longer serve us in adulthood. Recognizing a recurring fear as feedback on the location of an energy block is a huge step towards being free of fear. Allowing your fear to direct your actions is a surefire way to keep yourself rooted in a negative, unproductive state.

SCARCITY MENTALITY (mental/emotional)

A mindset of scarcity creates more scarcity. When we focus on not enough or limited resources then we are creating a scarcity mentality. Fear is the resulting emotion when the focus is on lack or scarcity. The emotion of fear vibrates at a very low level and it is very difficult to overcome even with the assistance of the strategies in the previous chapter. Alternately, a mindset of abundance creates more abundance. It is important to remember once again that we get what

> "Keep your face to the sunshine and you will not see the shadows."
>
> – Helen Keller

we focus on, so if your starting point is a focus on scarcity then your entire experience of life will be rooted in this scarcity. There will never be enough of anything to satisfy your needs and you will never feel truly safe.

It is absolutely essential for us to break the habit of rooting our energy in the concept of scarcity. It is easy to tell if we have this problem just by listening to our language. Is the glass half-empty or half-full? We need to flip the paradigm such that we are rooting our focus in the concept of abundance. The universe is infinitely abundant and there is more than enough of everything to go around. It might not appear that way, but remember that how we perceive the world is simply a reflection of our internal representation. If we change the internal representation, then the world suddenly shows up differently.

NEGATIVE MEDIA (mental)

Negativity in the media is at the top of the list of things

that can literally shift your focus from positive to negative in an instant. The majority of mainstream media is focused on bad news, disasters and glorified horror, all designed to engage us at our lowest level. Fear is one of the lowest vibrating emotions and carries with it a lot of power to hold us immobile. The mind employs the use of fear when it perceives the risk of action to be too high. Much of the mainstream media plays on this fear. Remember that people who are in a state of fear are very easy to control and direct.

An enormous amount of effort is required to shift out of the negative energy generated by the mainstream media. We spend a lot of precious energy countering the effects of the horrific images, dreadful descriptions and frightful sounds that accompany most mainstream media stories. The mainstream media is toxic to us and detrimental to our energy levels—plain and simple. The body must process this toxicity each and every time it encounters it, thus placing a huge strain on our physical systems.

> "Whoever controls the media, controls the mind."
> – Jim Morrison

It's not just the news that's negative. Note that advertisements are typically targeted at what's wrong. The majority of mainstream programming also plays out at the lowest level of emotions including excessive violence, hatred and intolerance. Rarely do we encounter uplifting stories of love, unity and peace. Consider that these types of stories are called "uplifting" because they raise our energetic vibration.

In 1999, the "Media Violence Inventory: A Parent's

Diary," produced by the YWCA of the U.S.A. stated that by the end of elementary school, most children have seen 8,000 murders and 100,000 other acts of violence on TV.[16] These numbers double by age 18. Is this what we really want for our children? Remember Dr. Emoto's research findings on the effects of negativity on the molecular structure of water. When water samples are bombarded with negative messages, the water does not form crystals at all and displays fragmented structures and chaos. Remember, our bodies are roughly 70 percent water. Don't you think the mainstream media is having the same effect on our children? On us?

Remember that what we focus on expands, even if it is something that we don't necessarily desire. The mainstream media focuses our attention on war, terrorism, panic and outbreaks. As a group this means that the collective consciousness is focusing on these horrible things. Guess what we will see more and more of if we continue to focus on these things? You got it—more war, terrorism, panic, outbreak.

The only way to break the cycle is to stop giving it our attention. Mother Teresa once said that she would not participate in an anti-war rally because the focus was still on war. She said that she would only participate in a peace rally because the focus is on peace. Where is your focus? Is it on what you want or what you don't want?

I know that there will be people out there who will say, "But I have to be informed; what choice do I have?" My

---

16   Huston, A.C., et al. *Big World, Small Screen: The Role of Television in American Society.* Lincoln: University of Nebraska Press, 1992.

question in response is, "Do you really need to know how many people died in a car accident halfway across the country?" Believe me, if a news story is important enough, you will find out about it. Besides, technology now allows you to find and filter the information that you need in the way that you need it. Why subject yourself to all the anxiety that accompanies bad news? Find another information outlet or demand that your mainstream media be delivered in a different format. Believe me when I tell you that the news is brought to us by the advertisers, and the advertisers need an audience. If the news audience disappeared because the news was bad for us, then the news network would do whatever it takes to bring that audience back. The audience, not the news network, holds the power. We have to take a stand for ourselves and our children on the negative effects the mainstream media is having on all of us.

BLAME (mental)

Laying blame keeps our focus on the external world and implies that there is something wrong out there. This simply cannot be if we understand that the outside world is just a reflection of our inside world. Remember that it is not the mirror's fault that you are having a bad hair day. The problem resides with your hair, not with the mirror's reflection of your hair. Blaming others is a futile waste of time and energy. However, blame can serve as a useful signal that your focus is on the reflection rather than on the source. When

> *"If you blame others for your failures, do you credit them with your success?"*
>
> *– Author unknown*

you notice that you have moved into blame, you are also able to understand that a simple shift to your inside world is all it will take to alter your outside world. Living is an inside-out process. You must look to your outside world for feedback about how you are progressing on the inside.

If you constantly find yourself blaming others, then you can use this to objectively observe your internal representation of the world. Remember that we cannot control the outside circumstances. When this is finally realized, the only thing left to do is to look inward for the peace and security that we are constantly demanding of our circumstances. Perhaps your internal representation of the world does not include the possibility of what you are looking for. An adjustment of your model of Reality is what is needed to bring you what you want. Consider that *when there is peace within there will be peace without.*

OBSTACLES (mental)

It is well known in the sport of downhill skiing that the easiest way to ski down a mountain covered in moguls is to find the straightest path between the moguls and focus on that path. If you focus on the size and number of the moguls, you'll be dead meat. It is the same in real life. We get what we focus on. If our focus is on obstacles, we will see obstacles at every turn. If our focus is on solutions, we will find the necessary resources to be able to handle and solve any problems that come our way.

There is a huge difference between problem-focused thinking and solution-focused thinking. When we focus on problems, we automatically look for more problems. You can see how this is not a good thing. Focusing on solutions causes us to look for more solutions. If you want to keep your energy levels high, you must be very mindful of which mindset you are empowering. There will always be obstacles in your path; the challenge is yours to determine how you will handle them. Things are usually hard for one of two reasons: either they are hard because you are being challenged to create a new state of Being or they are hard because you are going down a path that is incongruent to what you want. Only you ever know the source of your obstacles, so you must turn inward to determine what is right for you and then act upon it.

NEGATIVE SELF-TALK (mental/emotional)

Empowering that little voice in our heads that reinforces our negative beliefs is another habit that keeps us down. This is one of the most powerful sources of toxicity. These negative thoughts always lead to the most negative of emotions. Then the emotions reinforce the negative state, which leads to more negative thinking. We must do whatever it takes to break out of these self-defeating habits!

Sometimes breaking a habit can be as simple as shouting, "NO, THANK YOU!" when we notice the negative emotions present in our bodies or the thoughts in our heads. The purpose of doing this is to interrupt the pattern of negative self-talk. Once the pattern is interrupted, we can choose to replace it with something more positive and uplifting. Everyone suffers from some degree of self-doubt.

The problem arises when we give these thoughts our attention, even if we are trying to focus on not having them. We will get more of what we focus on. The best way to deal with this is to simply choose to remain in a state of gratitude for all our wonderful and redeeming qualities. We must learn to become masters of emotional self-awareness so that we can direct our emotions instead of letting them arise unconsciously.

GIVING UP (emotional)

Quitting is a guaranteed strategy for not getting what you want. Quitting is the direct result of empowering our doubts in our own abilities and the lowest levels of emotions that we have such as apathy and sadness. When we give up on a dream, we are effectively halting any momentum that we had in achieving it.

Most people give up at the most critical time in the pursuit, when holding on for just a little longer would produce the desired result. The quitting usually occurs at the very opportunistic point of maximum growth and change. This is usually preceded by a level of discomfort that is signaling the occurrence of a great change. This time is usually accompanied by

> *"He conquers who endures."*
> *– Persius*

unpleasant emotions, and the fear of merely experiencing these emotions can often be enough to cause a retreat. We sometimes don't realize that if we would just allow these emotions to pass and transform the energy associated with them, we could finally be free to receive that which we are seeking.

In chaos theory there is a term called bifurcation, which means "the place where something divides into two branches." Another term, perturbation, is defined as "disruption: the act of causing disorder." In 1977, Dr. Ilya Prigogine won the Nobel Prize in Chemistry for his works on dissipative structures. Dissipative structures are structures that are able to stay intact only because they exchange energy, matter or information from the surrounding environment.[17] Dissipative structures aren't limited to chemical solutions. The term can be widely applied to people, governments, cultures and

> "We turn to God for help when our foundations are shaking, only to learn it is God who is shaking them."
> – Charles C. West

school systems because they are systems that are capable of change and interaction with their environments. What Prigogine's work essentially led to was the understanding that when a dissipative system is exposed to perturbation, it eventually comes to a bifurcation point—the point at which the system is destroyed or is propelled to a new order of self-organization. In simple terms, it means that when we are under pressure we come to a point where we can retreat to safety or persevere and break through to a more powerful state of Being. In other words, chaos, disorder and instability can actually be the source of transformation to a higher functioning order.

---

17   Prigogine & Stengers, 1984.

The Process of Growth

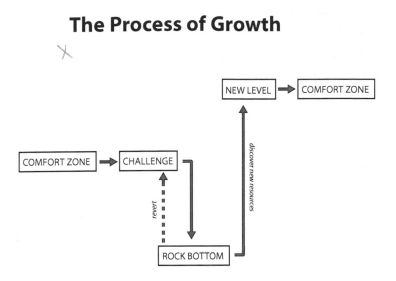

1. The comfort zone.
2. Challenge (perturbation) arises and the comfort zone is disturbed.
3. Rock bottom (the bifurcation point)—will you discover new resources allowing you to a new level of functioning or will you try to return to way it used to be in your original comfort zone?
4. New resources allow for an easy and effortless solution to the cause of the challenge (more complex functioning). You are at a new level.

1b. The new comfort zone and the process begins anew.

*Source: Adapted from The Change of State Indicator of Professor Clare Graves from SUNY, Schenectady, NY

Moving through to a more complex system (a more powerful state of Being) requires a leap of faith. It is not entirely clear what to hold on to and what to release in order to allow a new state of Being to emerge. If you find yourself in a cycle of giving up, this is a signal to watch for the point of retreat. The point of retreat is usually the point of greatest perturbation and often the act of holding on past this point leads to a breakthrough and the creation of a new state of Being. In the same way that diamonds are created from intense pressure and the reorganization of carbon atoms, you too are able to completely transform your state of Being by simply refusing to give up when things get hard. Instead, search for and find new ways of operating in the challenging situation. The refusal to capitulate to quitting usually provides the framework for the development of a new, more powerful state of Being that carries with it new and more powerful behaviors. As Winston Churchill once said, "Never, never, never, never give up."

My daughter has an incredible ability to stick with it. She does not give up easily at all. I remember when she was learning how to do a cartwheel. She wanted desperately to do a cartwheel because some of her friends could do them easily. As a former gymnast, I was excited that she had this same interest. However, her first attempt was more of a hand jump than a cartwheel. In her mind though, it was just *a cartwheel that needed some work*. She loved doing them. She did them all the time. They didn't look anything like cartwheels, but she kept doing them nonetheless. This went on for about a year. Whenever she had the chance and the space, she would practice her cartwheel. She would let me show her my cartwheel, she would watch her friends do cartwheels, she would draw pictures of herself doing cartwheels and she would continue to refine her cartwheel. She fell down a lot. She got quite dirty and even a little bruised. She could have easily quit and it wouldn't really have changed her life. But she kept at it. One day, almost two years after she started trying, I watched both of her legs come around in a fantastic cartwheel. It was one of the most exciting moments of my motherhood because I knew that the only reason why it happened was because she refused to quit, even though it seemed that it would never happen. She held on past this point and finally found the resources and the techniques that delivered an awesome cartwheel.

STAYING STUCK (mental/emotional)

Everyone gets stuck from time to time. This is normal. Getting stuck is not a problem; *staying* stuck is. Remember from Newton's First Law of Motion—an object at rest tends to stay at rest unless acted upon by an outside force. It takes a huge force to stop our momentum, but it also takes a huge force to get unstuck. If you can only keep moving, even just a little, you will find it easier to regain your speed. If you get stopped, you will need to expend a great deal more energy just to

> *"It does not matter how slowly you go, so long as you do not stop."*
> – Confucius

get moving in the right direction again. The longer you stay stuck, the more stuck you become and the more force you will need to get moving again. It is in your best interest to avoid staying stuck.

You can do this in a number of ways. Diverting your attention is usually one of the most effective ways to avoid staying stuck. Then, when your focus returns to the situation, you may have renewed energy and a little more perspective on how to keep moving. Another way to avoid staying stuck is to keep moving no matter what happens. This means that taking even the smallest of baby steps towards your goal is better than getting and staying stuck. You must find *something* you can accomplish and then do it. Remember your peak state anchors—this would be a great time to fire them off. Once you accomplish something, you need to celebrate your success. This way you refocus your energy on what you are doing well instead of on what you are doing wrong. If you do this enough times, you will find that you have built enough momentum to get moving again.

You will frequently be presented with the opportunity to choose between an action that supports your higher purpose and one that does not. At the end of the day, the responsibility to choose rests solely with you. The life you experience is a direct result of the choices you make about how to maintain your state of Being. Remember, the only thing you can do if you are not satisfied with your physical experience is to turn inwards and shift your state of Being.

THE BOTTOM LINE

Managing your state of Being is your responsibility. Your entire life experience flows from the starting point of your Being. You always have the choice to empower a positive, constructive state of Being. You also have a choice to empower a negative, destructive state of Being. In the end, it is always a choice. Negative states can be overcome, and it is most likely to happen when a powerful choice is made. The goal is to be mindful of the level of toxicity, emotional or physical, that we invite into our experiences. Their cumulative effect places a burden on the optimal functioning of our systems. If you do nothing else, then just be mindful of how much toxic stress that you put on your system and see if you can lessen the burden even just a little. This will go a long way in helping you to cultivate a peak performing state of Being.

"The drops of rain make a hole in the stone
not by violence but by oft falling."
— Lucretius

COMPANION ONLINE RESOURCE		THINK AGAIN!
		Visit www.GinaML.com/Chapters to get a summarized version of this chapter for your quick reference.

CHAPTER EIGHT

～～～～～

THE SIMPLE PROCESS

"Since everything in life is but an experience
perfect in being what it is, having nothing to do
with good or bad, acceptance or rejection,
one may well burst out in laughter."
– Long Chen Pa

The circumstances and events of the world are outside your control. That's not to say that individual action shouldn't have global perspective. However, in the end, the complexity and dynamic nature of external circumstances are not something that can be controlled by one person, even if one were to try really hard. In the end, the only thing that is really under your control is how you choose to respond to your circumstances. Your response is the only thing that is truly your own. You always have a choice when it comes to this response. You can cultivate your response with consciousness and awareness or you can allow your response to be dictated by past experiences and unconscious programming. Either way, it is a choice; your choice. If you don't exercise the power you have to choose this response, then you effectively give up your power in any situation. The situation doesn't render you powerless. Eleanor Roosevelt once said, "No one can make you feel inferior without your consent." You always have the power to choose your response. Giving up your choice is what actually robs you of your power in any situation.

The key to maintaining your power is to remain present to what is actually happening instead of giving in to the meaning created in your internal representation. Our unconscious responses to situations are either hardwired or created by years of habit. These unconscious responses can always be overridden, but they must become conscious again in order to do so. We must begin to bring our awareness to our responses as they are happening so that we can determine, objectively, if that response is appropriate to the present circumstance. The issue isn't the response itself. All responses serve a purpose in distinct situations. The issue is responding to a situation in an inappropriate manner with either an overreaction or an underreaction, based upon what is actually happening in the moment. These inappropriate responses wreak havoc on our bodies and in our relationships and ultimately stand between us and the life we really want to live.

EVERYBODY WANTS

In the end everybody just wants to be happy, to be loved and to feel safe. These are the basic human birthrights of joy, love and peace. No matter who you are, where you are at in your life, these are the basic desires. These desires may be covered up by years of suffering, disappointment, disillusionment and mistrust, but they are the core of who we are. Some of us may be way out of touch with these needs, mixing them up with the desire for material objects and/ or physical satisfaction. Others may be aware of the need for peace, love and joy but are completely baffled by how to achieve it. Others yet may be living fully in these experiences. There is no right answer and there is no right place to be. You start where you are and move forward from there. You can claim your birthright anytime you choose to because everything you are looking for is right in front of you. You just need to retrain yourself to see it.

> "There are only two ways to live your life. One is as though nothing is a miracle. The other is as though everything is a miracle."
>
> – Albert Einstein

Remember that we can only consciously process 126 bits of incoming information per second while there are millions of bits of information available. What we call "reality" is a mere fraction of what Reality actually is. What we call "reality" is only one potential version of the whole story, among almost infinite possibilities. Our task therefore is to choose our potential reality and to see if it works for us. It's as simple as choosing another potential version of reality and testing it out. In a sense, it's a game. The purpose of the game is to figure out which is the most powerful version of reality for our lives. We are on a mission to find the information that fills our life with peace, love and joy. Everything that we encounter along the way is part of the learning process. All of the circumstances that make up our life experience play a key part in helping us to determine what works and what doesn't work. Good and bad are an illusion of the mind. All circumstances serve your evolution, even if they don't feel good. All experiences play a critical role helping you to uncover the truth of who you are and what you are made of. Everything that happens is serving this evolution. In this context, it's all good.

We could all use more practice in learning to understand our circumstances as being feedback to this master game. If everything that is happening in our experience is serving to foster our growth and evolution, then it would follow that everything that happens is simply feedback to this process. We should learn how to use this feedback so that it enhances our life experiences and moves us further forward. Life is filled with content that is different for each and every person. However, life is also a process. This process is effectively the same for everybody. We should learn to become masters of the process of life instead of trying to control the content of life. Instead of focusing on the circumstances, we would be better served to learn how to optimize our response to the circumstances. This requires more effort on the process and less on the content except to understand how effectively we are responding to the circumstances. We always have control of our own individual process and how we respond within this process. We have much less control over the content of our lives, yet this is where we spend most of our energy. Perhaps it's time for a change.

THE FEEDBACK LOOP OF LIFE REVISITED

THE FEEDBACK LOOP OF LIFE

The process of life can be described as a simple feedback loop:

1. You have an idea of what you want (*being*)
2. You do some things (*doing*)
3. You either get it or you don't (*having*)

(When you don't get what you want, then you have some useful feedback that you can use to inform you on the next go-round.)

Obviously, the intricacies of life are much more complex than this, but in the big picture this is how it basically works. Everything that you have in your life is the ultimate result of the way you have been up until now. In this way, your results or your circumstances match a specific state of Being. If the cycle starts with your thoughts and feelings, then these are the true causes. Therefore, the results or circumstances are the effects of these causes. If you don't have what you want, then you have a choice to make: will you try to manipulate the circumstances in some way or will you choose powerful thoughts, physiology and emotions in response to the situation that will actually help you get where you want to go? If you decide to manage your response, then you have to go back to the source of the result and change the way you were Being. Change what you think and how you feel about it. What we do, the actions or behaviors that we carry out, are merely an intermediate step between the cause and the effect. While they are important to some degree they are not as important as we make them out to be. The biggest rewards come from focusing on achieving optimal ways or states of Being.

THE TWO MINDS

Why are some responses appropriate to the situation at hand and others completely inappropriate? What causes us to overreact or underreact to a situation? What drives our automatic default and sometimes hardwired responses? The answer is best explained using the concept that each of us has a conscious mind and an unconscious (or subconscious) mind.

The subject of conscious and unconscious mind is as old as antiquity. It has been studied, defined and redefined many times over. It has been the subject of debate in psychology, theology and science for years. Not everyone agrees with this distinction, however it provides a very useful analogy for understanding how and why people do the things that they do. There isn't an actual physical separation between the unconscious mind and the conscious mind. It is more of a description of how the functions are differentiated.

Think of your conscious mind as the part of you that we

call your "awareness" or your "attention." It is sequential and logical, responsible for your intellectual thinking and your self-talk or mind chatter; it is verbal. Your conscious mind can voluntarily move parts of your body. Your conscious mind contains your reasoning skills, your analytical skills and is the center for your cognitive learnings and understandings. It makes choices based on facts and directs your awareness when you are awake. The conscious mind is capable of processing the 126 bits of information per second,

> "The so-called miraculous powers of a great master are a natural accompaniment to his exact understanding of subtle laws that operate in the inner cosmos of consciousness."
>
> – Paramahansa Yogananda

as we have discussed throughout this book. The iceberg analogy has been used to describe the relationship between the conscious mind and the unconscious mind. Your conscious mind is said to be the tip of the iceberg that sticks out of the water.

The huge part of the iceberg that is hidden below the water is used to describe the unconscious mind. The unconscious mind has been described as the "power center" and operates below our level of our awareness. It controls our emotions and regulates all of the physiological functions of our bodies. For example, your unconscious mind is the part of you that keeps you breathing so you don't have to consciously remember to do it every time. Unlike your conscious mind, your unconscious mind multitasks and processes many events simultaneously. It is non-linear and can make associations between many ideas, feelings and thoughts at once. It has been shown that the unconscious mind can process more information more quickly than the conscious mind meaning that it can likely handle much more than 126 bits of information per second.[18] In this sense, the unconscious mind is seen to attend to the overwhelming amount of stimuli around us so that the conscious mind can focus on what's important and make quick decisions. The unconscious mind is responsible for much of the deleting, distorting and generalizing that goes on when we try to form an internal representation of reality. All of our memories and past experiences are stored in our unconscious mind and it decides which of these memories will be available to us in our conscious mind.

An interesting quality of the unconscious mind is that it does not recognize negatives and has no ability to reject. If the unconscious mind is repeatedly told by the conscious mind that something is true, then it accepts this suggestion without bias. If you use language such as, "Don't forget to do your homework," then your unconscious mind can only hear the command as, "Forget to do your homework," because it cannot process the negation "don't." Dr. Joseph Murphy, a pioneer in the description of the subconscious mind used an analogy of the unconscious mind as the darkroom in which we develop the images to be lived out in real life. Aside from running the body, the unconscious mind does not initiate action—it merely carries out directions from the conscious

18   "Fleeting Images of Fearful Faces Reveal Neurocircuitry of Unconscious Anxiety by Columbia University." www.medicalnewstoday. com. December 18, 2004.

mind to produce action. That being said, when a conscious mind process becomes so efficient, repetitive and predictable it moves out of our conscious awareness. In this instance, it will run unconsciously, however, it technically remains a conscious mind process.

Change, therefore, is the result of redirecting both our conscious mind and our unconscious mind. It has been said that the conscious mind is the goal **setter**, but the unconscious mind is the goal **getter**. By observing our response to any situation we can make the unconscious aspects of that response part of our conscious awareness. In doing so, we can begin to understand how we are actually operating from a holistic point of view. We can start to see the whole picture and begin to pinpoint situations where our conscious mind has been giving mixed messages to our unconscious mind. By understanding how our mind works and how to use the feedback that we are getting, we can begin to literally create the life of our dreams. I have developed a simple process for making your unconscious processes part of your conscious awareness so that you can finally change them for your advantage. This is done by using the feedback inherent in your circumstances to make the necessary changes in your state of Being (thoughts and feelings) so that you can direct your life in the direction that you want it to go.

GETTING WHAT YOU WANT

The process for getting what you want is quite simple, but often not easy. The difficulty lies in the fact that we must become responsible for shaping our life experience. In accepting this responsibility, we give up the ability to blame our life experience on anyone or anything on the outside. For many people this can be a daunting concept. However, once you get over this hurdle you can begin to craft the life experience that you were born to live. The Simple Process is about taking the feedback contained in your circumstances and using it to understand what you are actually looking for. It looks like this:

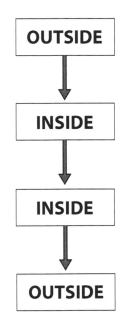

OUTSIDE—THE RESULT

Most people have no trouble looking to the outside for answers. Most people base the quality of their lives and their self-esteem on their results and their circumstances. Most people look to the outside to understand how they are measuring up. The issue is that your external circumstances have nothing to do with who you are or even how capable you are. Your circumstances merely reflect who you set out to Be at the beginning of the feedback cycle. Your results actually contain all of the information that you need to get what you want. However, most of us have never been trained to look at it that way before.

The external circumstance is a data point. You either get what you want or you don't. In either case, you get feedback. When the result is not what was originally intended it indicates that there was an incongruity between the conscious mind and the unconscious mind. It means that even though you decided that you wanted something consciously, there was a mix-up in your directions at the unconscious level that led to the unsuccessful result. In short, it means that there was a discrepancy between your present thinking and your actual neurological behavior (responses). Usually it means that the unconscious mind is operating with longstanding instructions that contradict and override the new ideas being put forth by the conscious mind. Remember that your unconscious mind houses all of your memories, past experiences, as well as your beliefs and values. These are built up over years of conditioning and repetition. The unconscious mind does not have the ability to reject so it creates a reality based on these habitual thought

> *"If you think your whole life is going wrong just because so much of it is going wrong, then you're wrong. Mostly when things go wrong, they're meant to go wrong, so we can outgrow what we have to outgrow."*
>
> *– Author unknown*

and emotional patterns. If you suddenly introduce an idea that contradicts these longstanding habitual responses, then it stands to reason that while your unconscious mind will accept the idea, it won't be sufficient to overturn the preexisting determinants of your behavior. The unconscious mind requires a lot of repetition in order to install a new neurological behavior.

When repetitively told by the conscious mind that something is true, the unconscious mind will assemble all of its resources in order to act according to the direction of the conscious mind. For example, if the conscious mind consistently holds the thought that all deadlines are stressful, the unconscious mind will produce a stress response. After many repetitions, this response will eventually become an unconscious process that is activated anytime you encounter a deadline, even if the specific deadline in question is in no way stressful (e.g. buying a birthday present before the birthday party). The unconscious mind cannot distinguish between an appropriate response and an inappropriate response; it merely provides the response that has been conditioned to go with a situation.

If you are not conscious of this mechanism, then you will never make the distinction between an appropriate response and one that does not fit the actual circumstances. Only in bringing this mechanism into your conscious awareness do you now have the ability to determine which response would be most appropriate. The easiest way to determine whether you have a discrepancy between your conscious mind and your unconscious mind is to look at your results or your circumstances. **If you have anything other than what you want, then it indicates a discrepancy.** Your job then is to discover the source of the discrepancy and rectify it. This is how you use your results as feedback. The circumstances never lie. You need to be honest with yourself as to where you really are.

INSIDE—THE REAL WANTING

This is where the process goes internal. You need to turn inward to rectify this discrepancy and uncover the unconscious parts of your process. The first thing you need to do is examine what it is you said you wanted. What is the result that you wanted but don't have? The question you must ask yourself is: "Why do I want that?"

This process is best illustrated with an example from a volunteer named Rick that I worked with in one of my seminars. In this case, the volunteer said he wanted to have a new deck for his house, but it just wasn't happening. Here is how the process went:

> ME: "Why do you want this new deck?"
> RICK: "So I can enjoy being outside."
> ME: "Why do you want to enjoy being outside?"
> RICK: "So I can relax and spend time with my family."
> ME: "Why do you want to relax and spend time with your family?"
> RICK: "So I can be around them more."
> ME: "Why do you want to be around them more?"
> RICK: "So I can be loved."

Ultimately, what this man wanted was to *be loved* and he was using the notion that if he only had the deck, then he would be loved. But this is HAVE-DO-BE thinking and it's backwards as we all now know. However, he just brought a very important bit of information into his conscious awareness by going through this process. He learned that what he is really looking for right now is love. The lack of the deck was really highlighting the lack of love in that moment. Love is his *real* wanting, not the deck. This is not to say that he isn't loved or hasn't been loved, but what it shows is that right now, in the present moment, he is *not feeling loved* but wants to be. The lack of something always points the way to the *real* wanting. You just have to ask yourself, "Why?" and keep asking until you get there. A *real* wanting is always a state of Being and usually falls into the categories or subsets of peace, love or joy, for this is ultimately what anybody really wants.

INSIDE—THE SHIFT

Once you have discovered your *real* wanting, then you have a choice. Will you continue to allow your unconscious responses to dictate your behavior to the circumstances or will you claim the power you have to direct your response in a powerful way? Will you claim your power to *think* before you act? Seeing beyond your circumstances to your *real*

> "It doesn't work to leap a 20-foot chasm in two 10-foot jumps."
>
> – American proverb

wanting is the gateway to making a powerful choice. When you discover what you really want, then you can decide to choose that for yourself. Being is always a choice. You can choose to create a state of Being that is powerful or you can allow your state of Being to be dictated by your default, habitual and programmed responses. The choice is always yours. If you decide to claim the power you have to choose your state of Being, then you will be on your way to initiating a new cycle of cause and effect. A new state of Being will always bring about a new experience.

Let's use an example of something we all want: happiness (which happens to be another way to say "joy"). Happiness is a choice. It is not given to you by someone or something else. It is chosen by you as a state of Being. Many people have trouble at this point in trying to conjure up happiness. One of the fastest ways to reconnect with a state of Being is to remember a time when you were Being it, in this case Being happy. I discovered a very valuable insight when I was writing the word "remember" on a flipchart during a seminar. I wrote it this way, which triggered the insight:

Re-member

"Re" as in "again."

"Member" as in "limb or body part."

I was struck with the realization that a key factor in recalling memories was actually bringing the experience back into our body parts. The etymological origin of the word "remember" is from the Latin *rememorari*, which can be broken down as:

"Re" as in "*again*."

"Memorari" as in "*mindful.*"

The origin of the word "remember" means *to be mindful again.* We usually associate the word "mindful" with only our thinking mind: our conscious mind. However, recall that the mind also contains our unconscious mind: our feeling mind. Therefore, when we remember something we should not only think about it again but we should also *feel it* again. This is the key to accessing what you are looking for. When you think back to a time when you were Being happy, then you have to re-create the whole experience. You need to bring back the sights, sounds, feelings, smells, tastes and the description of the event. You need to bring back the entire internal representation in order to really have access to the entire state of Being happy. It's not enough to just think about it. You have to bring back the whole picture and hold it in your mind <u>and</u> your body. All aspects of the internal representation must be congruent.

Now that you have the entire representation of what it means to be happy, you can choose to make that representation part of the present situation. You can choose to BE happy right now by using the memory of Being happy as the blueprint. What thoughts are going though your head? Where do you feel it in your body? Can you hold the thoughts and the feelings in the same way that you would hold a note if you were singing a song? Rev. Dr. Michael Bernard Beckwith has referred to these experiences as "feeling tones." In the same way that you can hum a tone, you can learn to hold a feeling tone. The longer that you are able to hold the tone, the stronger you get in generating that state of Being. You bring your knowledge of Being happy into your conscious awareness. You choose to be happy instead of allowing your choice to be dictated by past experiences and programming. This shift must occur inside you. Nothing on the outside can cause this shift to happen. You must choose it.

There's another step that you must take in helping to manifest the life that you want. You must learn to retrain your unconscious mind as to what you really want and believe. You need to undo the unconscious responses and programming that are getting in the way of what you want. There are two main ways to do this. You can go to the unconscious mind directly and replace these responses with new empowering models. This is usually done with some type of therapist or coach who guides you at the unconscious level to optimize your model of the world. There are a number of therapies that have been designed to bypass the critical thinking and judging of the conscious mind and work directly at the unconscious level. These changes are often profound and well worth the research and effort to find the right one. In my experience the combined techniques of NLP, Hypnotherapy and Time Line Therapy® are very effective at producing result through unconscious conscious integration.

> "Man is made by his belief. As he believes, so he is."
>
> – Bhagavad Gita

Another way to effect change at the unconscious level involves using your conscious mind. Remember that the unconscious mind will accept whatever the conscious mind tells it and that it cannot process negatives. If you repeatedly impress an idea upon the unconscious mind, then it will reorganize all of the resources needed to make that idea a reality. The way to do this is to create an affirmation in the form of an idea in the conscious mind and then to repeatedly impress this idea on your unconscious mind. An effective affirmation must have the following qualities:

- It must be stated in the positive. You must focus on what you want instead of what you don't want. The easiest way to do this is to write down what you do <u>not</u> want and then rewrite the <u>exact opposite</u> stated in positive terms.

- It must be stated in the present tense. If you tell your unconscious mind that you "want money," then it will present a model that "wants money." Whereas if you tell it that you "have money," then it will reorganize your resources so that you actually "have" the money. The difference in the language is very important.

- It must be as detailed as possible. The unconscious mind is literal so you need be very specific in giving it directions.

Often times, the best affirmations are created by using the Mirror Principle when you are taking stock of your current situation. For example, let's say you have a boss that is always giving you work on Friday at four o'clock in the afternoon that he wants to see first thing Monday morning. You might say to yourself or a friend "My boss is always giving me work at the last minute. He just doesn't respect me." Let's use the Mirror Principle here and shift the sentence, "*He just doesn't respect me*" to "*I just don't respect myself.*" Hmmm. Could there be a shred of truth there? My guess is that it's more than a shred and if turn it into a positive statement like "I do respect myself" and use this derived observation as your affirmation, you will see a profound shift in your life. Remember that the circumstances and people in our lives are merely a reflection of who we are at the deepest level. Learning to repect yourself in the case of our example is likely at the source of much angst.

Another way to develop a powerful affirmation is to make a list of what you don't want and then flip it over 100 percent. Just take everything you don't want and write the exact opposite. That's a quick way to get around any resistance that you might have to actually getting and having what you want.

In the end, you will have created an effective affirmation that you can begin using to recondition your unconscious mind. You make this affirmation incredibly powerful when you connect it with the internal representation of the state of Being that you identified as the *real* wanting. It is the combination of these two steps that brings about new outcomes in your circumstances. Both steps require a choice; a choice by you to take control of your responses so that your circumstances don't get control of you.

OUTSIDE—THE NEW REALITY

The final step is to bring this internal shift into your reality. This is done by repetition and practice. This is why there is a temporary reality between the potential reality and the physical reality; it takes time for the unconscious mind to develop a new habit. You must repeat, repeat and repeat some more. It means taking your affirmation and marrying it with your powerful state of Being and repeating it over and over again. The key to the affirmation is to ensure that it is filled with emotion, sights, sounds, smells and tastes. The thought of your affirmation comes alive with the feelings of your internal representation. These two lead to new behaviors that set you on a course for new outcomes. You must take action towards what you want. Given that you have made changes on the level of "cause," you can now expect a new "effect" to emerge as a result of your new choices. When this new "effect" or result becomes apparent to you, then you will have more information. Either you will get what you said you wanted or you will not. If you don't get what you want, guess what? You get *feedback*. You will have just uncovered another unconscious part of your process. You can then take this feedback and use it to inform The Simple Process once again.

Remember, I said it was simple, not easy. The challenge comes when you do not get the results you want. At this point you have a choice—you can quit and return to your unconscious, habitual responses or you can choose to try again. The reason why you do not have what you want is the disconnect between your conscious mind and your unconscious mind. Your neurology has not caught up with your thinking. It is up to you to find this disconnect. The answers are always in front of you, contained in the feedback inherent in your circumstances. You can choose to

> *"There is nothing I can tell you that you do not already know. There is no question that you can ask me that you yourself cannot answer. You have just forgotten."*
>
> *– David Littlewood*

explore this feedback and look deeper into yourself for the answers or you can choose to remain oblivious to your power. If you choose to look deeper within yourself you will find outdated beliefs, habits, values and responses that no longer serve you. Your job is to weed out anything that doesn't serve you and replace it with powerful states of Being. The process is cyclical and continuous, and it is vital to your growth and evolution. It's not about controlling the circumstances. It's about understanding your responses and your ability to direct your responses.

THE SIMPLE PROCESS IN A NUTSHELL

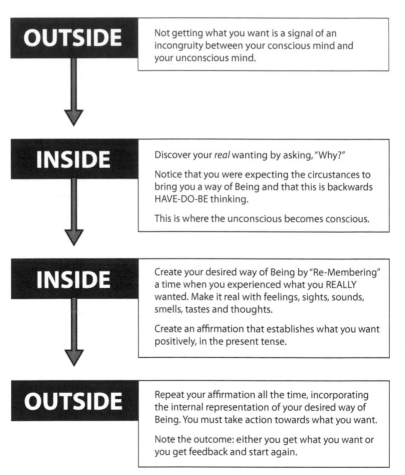

OUTSIDE

Not getting what you want is a signal of an incongruity between your conscious mind and your unconscious mind.

INSIDE

Discover your *real* wanting by asking, "Why?"

Notice that you were expecting the circustances to bring you a way of Being and that this is backwards HAVE-DO-BE thinking.

This is where the unconscious becomes conscious.

INSIDE

Create your desired way of Being by "Re-Membering" a time when you experienced what you REALLY wanted. Make it real with feelings, sights, sounds, smells, tastes and thoughts.

Create an affirmation that establishes what you want positively, in the present tense.

OUTSIDE

Repeat your affirmation all the time, incorporating the internal representation of your desired way of Being. You must take action towards what you want.

Note the outcome: either you get what you want or you get feedback and start again.

THE SIMPLE PROCESS

Use a real example from your life to illustrate this process for you.

What do you want that you don't have? Choose something easy to work with. _____

_____

Why do you want it? What is your real wanting? _____

_____

_____

Can you "Re-Member" a time when you were that state of Being? Think of a specific time and bring it back into your body.

What did you see, hear, smell, taste?_____

_____

How did you feel?_____

_____

What were your thoughts?_____

_____

_____

Take a moment to really hold onto that experience as if it were happening all over again. Hold the feeling tone.

Create an affirmation that reprograms your thinking (use the Mirror Principle or use what you don't want as a guide to what you want). _____

_____

_____

Repeat your affirmation and combine it with your "re-membered" state of Being. Take actions towards what you want. Do this many times a day. Observe what happens.

DESTINY

You may have heard someone say, "It just wasn't meant to be." This is true to the extent that the outcome didn't match the conscious desire. However, we know that it wasn't meant to be because there was a misalignment in our mind. Destiny is not something that is predetermined before we are born and we therefore have no impact on it. What we call "destiny" is simply a way of justifying the act of giving up when faced with undesired circumstances. If we chalk it up to destiny, then it's not our fault. We abdicate the responsibility for our happiness to some force out there instead of claiming the power to choose our responses and ultimately shape our destiny.

Another commonly held belief about destiny is that there is some grand plan for each of us, determined by a higher power and completely detached from us. In this scenario, we plug along in life, accepting our fate as truth and as something we have no influence over. Each and every disappointment is dismissed as "not part of my path," so that instead of learning and growing through our failures, we just perpetuate our misery. There may be some truth to the notion that we have come to this earth to learn specific lessons for our spiritual growth. However, we have our own free will to determine if, how and when we learn these lessons.

Life is not preordained, running out its course while we suffer the inevitable. We are creating our lives every single day, every single minute. In each moment, we have the creative power to completely alter the outcome. Anything we want is absolutely within our reach.

If you are <u>not</u> getting what you want, you are creating some type of block at the unconscious level to ensure that you do not receive it. If you are <u>not</u> getting what you want, you need to take a moment to consider the feedback and then <u>use it</u> to your advantage. You must search out the blocks, deal with them and create new ways of Being that bring about the life you want to live.

MIRACLES

Even though it seems as though this book is full of practical advice, it is also equally representative of many unseen processes. Consider for a moment that there are things we simply do not understand about this world. Just be open to that possibility. How do you explain the inexplicable? Should you accept it, ignore it or dismiss it? What if you could allow for it? What would be possible for you if the impossible were completely possible? What career might you have? What relationships would you enjoy? What disease could you cure?

> *"The invariable mark of wisdom is to see the miraculous in the common."*
>
> *– Ralph Waldo Emerson*

There have been countless documented cases of utterly inexplicable things happening since the beginning of time. These mysteries provide insight into the awesome power of the Universe and shed light on the vast array of information that is simply not understood. Did Jesus really walk on water? Did Norman Cousins really save his own life simply by laughing? Did that blind man teach himself to see? Can people really levitate? Does a psychic really read minds? Is there such a thing as a fairy? Can children really see angels? What if all of it really happened? What does that mean for everything we consider impossible?

If you can believe in miracles, you might be able to see that anything is possible. Remember that faith is about believing in something without having any proof. You will also recall that the mind cannot tell the difference between the visualization of something and its physical occurrence. If you can visualize something that once seemed impossible and then have faith that everything is possible, you'll see how it is quite conceivable that that thing just might come about. That's all it takes, and it starts with the belief. Physical reality will always align with potential reality. Always. What would you do if you *knew* you could do it?

AUTHENTICITY

The rest of this chapter is dedicated to helping you reach for *your* stars and create a life that you absolutely love, using the techniques outlined in this book. This is not the place to play small and accept sensible options. This is your chance to play big and to reclaim your enthusiasm for life. What would you attempt if you *knew* your success was guaranteed? What would you do if you knew you only had one year left to live? Life is meant to be lived vigorously. We tend to regret the thing we wished that we had done.

I believe that everyone has a unique purpose and a distinct gift to give the rest of the world. I also believe that each one of us creates the perfect scenario in which to deliver this gift, all the while learning the lessons that need to be learned. Your commitment to your higher purpose will give you the strength to continue when confronted with challenges and obstacles. Your vision for contributing to others will give you energy when you get stopped and stuck in your own story. Being clear about your purpose and the contribution you can make to others is integral to getting the most out of life. Your vision must be YOUR vision, coming from deep inside you.

> *"If you call forth what is in you, it will save you. If you do not call forth what is in you, it will destroy you."*
>
> *– Gospel of Saint Thomas*

Have you ever seen those little plastic puzzles where the pieces all move around to create a big picture? I use these puzzles in my seminars and speeches to illustrate that though each of us is unique, we are all part of the same big picture. When the pieces are in their correct location, the picture works. However, when even just one piece is out of place, the picture doesn't work and there is chaos in the puzzle. It is the same thing in real life. Each of us must find our place in the big picture. You must find your place. There isn't a better or more important place. There is only *your* place. There is only *your* path. There is only right now.

42-DAY PROJECTS

Forty-two-day projects are an excellent way to play the game of life. They are long enough to allow us to accomplish something, but short enough to maintain our attention. The number 42 also holds a little significance. It takes 21 days to create a habit and another 21 days to master it. Also, according to *The Hitchhiker's Guide to the Galaxy*, the answer to "life, the universe and everything is 42." I like this reason the best simply because it's funny. There is something serendipitous about the number 42, so I created the "42-day project." This technique gives us a chance to observe the Feedback Loop of Life and create a life we love.

There are four steps to the 42-day project:
1. BE
2. DO
3. HAVE
4. REPEAT for 42 days

Be

What do you want to have? This step is where you choose a potential reality. What is a powerful state of Being? You must describe this potential reality in as much detail as possible, in the present tense, as if you are really experiencing it. Your state of Being is made up of mental, emotional and physical components. Your focus is determined by your internal representation of the world. This includes the sights, sounds, feelings, smells and tastes along with your description of reality. You will know you are complete with this step when you have a clear picture in your mind of your finish line. The unconscious mind loves pictures and symbols, so this is a really important step. This will also help you recognize it when you get there.

Do

Once you have a clear picture of your finish line, you need to fill your time with inspired action. The "doing" phase is a temporary reality whereby your unconscious mind is reorganizing your resources. During this temporary reality, there is an opportunity to create an inspired action plan. It is important that this plan starts with the end in mind (i.e., our finish line). You can then begin to break down your finish line into generations of goal babies until you have a manageable list of things to do on a daily basis. Your actions will be congruent to your state of Being, so it is important to be mindful of your state of Being. If you find yourself slipping out of a peak performance state, then use one of the handles outlined in chapter six to help put you back on track. The key to inspired action is that it flows from your affirmation and your powerful state of Being. This phase is the realm of faith. Trust the process and keep moving forward. Repetition is the key when you are trying to create a new habit. Do your affirmations, take action and maintain focus on what you want.

Have

There will come a point in time where you will either get what you want or get feedback. If you get what you want, then you need to be sure to celebrate your success and enjoy the fruits of your labor. If you get feedback instead of getting what you want, you need to take the time to understand the feedback and learn from it. Observe what it is that you get and use The Simple Process for interpreting this feedback to create a new state of Being that is aligned with what you want.

Repeat

If you got feedback instead of what you wanted, then this

would be the right time to adjust your state of Being and give it another try. You must BE something different. This will ensure a different result. Whatever you get, you must continue to repeat the process for 42 days.

I used to be an avid athlete. At the high school varsity level, I played basketball, volleyball, soccer, track and field and my favorite: gymnastics. At the club level, I coached swimming, diving, gymnastics, soccer and basketball. At the university level, I was a varsity rower and an enthusiastic intramural athlete. I have done triathlons and marathons, and I have hiked all over the world. However, there was a point after having two children that I was out of shape, unable to do one regular sit-up. Instead of getting upset about this fact, I decided to turn it into a 42-day project. I decided to make it fun and social and joined an outdoor boot camp class that met early in the morning near my house. The first day was abysmal, no sit-ups. However, they gave me some tips and I stayed focused. After about 14 days, I was able to do a sit-up, but it was far from pretty and I still cheated a little. Each day my strength and abilities got stronger as my body began to rebuild the old neural networks. By the end of the 42 days, I was a veritable sit-up machine. It was a fun way to focus on creating a new habit that felt more like a challenge than a boring task. By giving myself 42 days to accomplish it, I allowed myself enough time to try a few different approaches and attempts before I judged my final result. This is obviously a fun little example, but I have used the same principle of 42-day projects to achieve outcomes such as writing a book, organizing my first conference and even rekindling my romance and connection to my husband. Forty-two-day projects make it fun.

A VISION AND A CHALLENGE

If anything were possible, what would you wish for? Imagine a world in which each person is living completely aligned with her or his true self and higher purpose, in harmony with every other creature on the planet. Close your eyes and just imagine it. This is what I am envisioning every chance I get. It begins by mastering the potential reality within myself, so that I will come to see it in the physical world. Until that time, I will continue to use the feedback I get to refine the process. What gets me out of bed in the morning is my commitment to reveal greatness. This is the umbrella under which I do everything whether it is writing, speaking, training, coaching, running my companies, parenting or even just walking down the boardwalk. It's who I am.

I have always been moved by the following passage from *A Return to Love* by Marianne Williamson. Nelson Mandela decided to use it in his 1994 inaugural speech when he was given the trust and confidence to rebuild the nation of South Africa. I use this powerful passage in my workshops. You can also download a beautifully formatted version of it from my website www.GinaML.com.

From *A Return to Love*

Our deepest fear is not that we are inadequate.
Our deepest fear is that we are powerful beyond measure.
It is our light, not our darkness, that most frightens us.
We ask ourselves, 'Who am I to be brilliant, gorgeous,
talented and fabulous?'
Actually, who are you not to be?
Your playing small doesn't serve the world. There is
nothing enlightened about shrinking so that others won't
feel insecure around you.
We were born to make manifest the glory that is within us.
It's not just in us, it's in everyone.
As we let our own light shine, we unconsciously give
others permission to do the same.
As we are liberated from fear, our presence automatically
liberates others.

– Marianne Williamson

We are here to make manifest the glory that is within us. We are here to make a difference in this world. If you are wondering if this is the time that you should be doing something, all you need to do is look around. You are alive now, so now is the time. Every single person has a unique gift to give to humanity, and humanity is begging for those gifts. Everywhere we turn, people are in need, pleading for our gifts.

It can be frightening to let your light shine. It can be terrifying to expose your true self for everyone to see. But you will suffer if you continue to suppress your true self and higher purpose. Your spirit will suffer from lack of expression. Your soul will suffer from lack of freedom. This in and of itself is a tragedy. But this is not the worst tragedy.

People everywhere could suffer if you continue to suppress your true self and higher purpose. People everywhere could suffer if you keep your spirit hidden and your soul locked up. It's not just about *you*; it's about this whole world. You will never realize the impact that you can have unless you make it. No one ever reveres what doesn't get done. Humanity is always grateful for what does get done.

If not now, when?

If not you, who?

THINK OR SINK

At the end of day, it comes down to a choice. The choice is always yours to make. If you don't make the choice then a choice will be made for you unconsciously. There will always be undesired circumstances. There will always be situations that we'd rather not experience. We cannot control these external events. The only control we have, the only control we've ever had, is our own internal response. Instead of expecting, hoping and demanding that our circumstances change so that we can finally be happy, loved and secure, we can direct that energy to finding out how we can create those realities within us regardless of the circumstances. This is true power; knowing that you can create a state of peace, love or joy at any moment. So, what's it going to be? Will you choose to think consciously and find a powerful state of Being or will you sink into your default, habitual preprogrammed responses? The choice is always yours.

> *"If you deliberately plan on being less than you*
> *are capable of being, then I warn you that*
> *you'll be unhappy for the rest of your life."*
> *– Abraham H. Malsow*

COMPANION ONLINE RESOURCE	THINK AGAIN!
	Visit www.GinaML.com/Chapters to get a summarized version of this chapter for your quick reference.

CHAPTER NINE

~~~~~~~~~~

42 THINGS THAT WILL
HELP YOU SHIFT

"We either make ourselves miserable,
or we make ourselves strong.
The amount of work is the same."
– Carlos Castaneda

This chapter is dedicated to helping you create shifts in your state of Being. Each item on this list will affect a mental, emotional or physical component or a combination thereof. These shifts will always serve to uplevel your state of Being into a more powerful state. When you make these shifts you will find that you reveal more choices and options for how you will respond in any situation. Keep this list handy for times when you need an extra boost.

1. Breathe.
Remember to breathe deeply and slowly with your diaphragm. You are aiming for 5–6 breaths per minute for optimal function. Each breath should allow your lungs to expand downward thus causing your belly to move outwards. Your chest should remain still during your breathing.

2. Keep a journal.
Make sure you write in it. You never know when the insight from a previous day will come in handy. Record your feelings as well as your thoughts. Buy journals that inspire you instead of the plain black ones with lined pages. Include a section on gratitude—it will keep you focused in the right direction.

3. Celebrate one success every single day.
Do not let yourself fall asleep without celebrating something you accomplished that day. Even if you can only produce freshly cleaned teeth, give it your best hoot-and-holler. It is important to be enthusiastic when celebrating your successes. You cannot overdo this enthusiasm—the more, the better.

4. Make a list of 100 things you want to do before you die.
Start doing them tomorrow. Check them off as you accomplish them. Try to do one thing on your list every year on your birthday. Review the list at least once a year and add to it as necessary. Record your adventures in your journal. Take a picture of yourself doing each thing. You need to know what you love to do.

5. Read inspiring quotes.
Read at least one insight every day. Subscribe to a service that delivers a quote to your inbox every day. I send one out every day. Check it out at www.GinaML.com. Recognize the wisdom in the quote you receive on any given day. Try to understand this wisdom and apply it throughout your day.

Write your own quotes. Publish them.

6. Surround yourself with color.
Every color has its own vibration and affects your moods. Pick a color of the day. Try to wear it, eat it, drink it and notice it everywhere. Write with coloured ink and on colored paper. Dream in color. Surround yourself with color.

7. Give at least one hug every single day.
Make sure you hug heart-to-heart so that your heart is touching the heart of the other person. Be firm with your hug—no wishy-washy hugs allowed. Try giving hugs instead of shaking hands with the new people you meet.

8. Say "I love you" to the image in your mirror every morning.
You can also include "good morning" and "you're beautiful." This is an excellent way to start your day and to remind yourself that you are responsible for loving yourself. You must impress this belief upon your unconscious mind. Do it often.

9. Say "I love you" to someone else every single day.
Try to pick a different person every day. Be sincere. Look them in the eye. Feel your heart reaching out to theirs. Say it to people who least expect it.

10. Perform random, anonymous acts of kindness.
Try to do something kind for someone every day. Make sure they do not know it was you. Take pleasure in the fact that they are trying to figure out who did it. If someone finds you out,

encourage them to pay it forward to performing another act of kindness for someone else.

11. Pick up every single penny you find and bless it.
Consider it a gift when you find money on the ground. Demonstrate that you are ready to accept any and all money that comes your way. Put that money towards your financial freedom.

12. Make a list of everything you are grateful for and carry it with you.
Update the list as often as you can, especially when you are feeling down. Read the list every time you need to boost your energy. Record the list in your voice and listen to it while you work out or drive your car.

13. Talk to strangers.
Remember that your reality is a projection. This person represents a part of you. Find out why he or she is in your life. Ask questions. Listen for the answers. See the light in each and every person you meet.

14. Sing out loud every day.
Do it in the shower or in the car. Test the range of your vocal chords. Imitate your favorite performers. Play air guitar or air drums. Do it with enthusiasm. Always sing to your children. Always sing with your children. Always sing your national anthem.

15. Dance every single day.
Do it while you are getting dressed or whenever you hear a

catchy beat. Tap your toes whenever you can. Wiggle your hips. Always dance with your children. Take your spouse for a twirl when you get home from work. Always dance at weddings. Dancing changes your physiology in a very magical way.

16. Meditate every day.

Find a meditation technique that works for you and practice it. Give yourself some time to quiet your mind. You deserve to connect with your reality without any conscious description. You deserve to feel what is really there.

17. Listen to beautiful music.

Explore different types of music and how they make you feel. Stick with the ones that give you warm fuzzies. Remember that people like Mozart and Beethoven are considered geniuses for a reason.

18. Do one thing every day that scares you.

It can be anything, even talking to someone you don't know. Be sure to look for the opportunity to do something scary. Remember, scary for you does not mean scary for someone else. You will know when you are scared. Recognize it, acknowledge it and then do it anyway. This will retrain your unconscious response to fear as one that includes action towards your goals.

19. Play at 100 percent and expect zero percent.

Give your full effort every single time you do something. Never hold back, especially your enthusiasm. If you don't expect anything in return, you'll never be disappointed.

20. Train yourself to enjoy something you don't currently like.
My husband taught me this trick. He taught himself to like things like olives and coffee this way. Think of it as a game. You can really expand your comfort zone with this one. New opportunities open up when you constantly expand your horizons.

21. Remember other people's birthdays.
Most people crave acknowledgement and attention. Show other people that you notice them by remembering their birthday. Use your computer software to remind you when their special day arrives. Send an email, an e-card or make a phone call. It makes a world of difference.

22. Remember other people's names.
Do whatever it takes to remember someone's name when you meet them. Devise a system and use it. Test yourself. Commit yourself to remembering his or her name. This forces you to be fully present in the moment.

23. Model successful people.
Look for people that inspire you. Notice how they do things. Copy their actions. Try to understand who they are Being and then recreate that for yourself.

24. Take the "im" out of im*possible* at least once a year.
Make a list of things that are im*possible* for you. Put the list on your bulletin board. Choose one thing each year to knock off your list and watch as your realm of *possibility* grows.

25. Laugh every single day.

Laughter really is the best medicine. Watch funny movies. Get a joke-of-the-day book or calendar. Tell jokes. Read funny books and comics. Listen to people's funny stories. Laughter oxygenates your blood and floods your system with endorphins.

26. Constantly remind your children that you believe in them.

Make it a point to tell your children every single day that "they can do it"—no matter how small their task may appear. Reflect to them this belief so that they will begin to identify it as their own. You can't impress this enough on their little unconscious minds.

27. Stand up for what you believe in.

Know what is important to you. State your beliefs firmly, avoiding confrontation. Disregard the need to please everyone and remain focused in your integrity. Taking a stand allows others the courage to do the same.

28. Accept your parents for who they are.

Your parents did the best they could with what they had. You will come to understand this if you have your own children. Recognize that there are no accidents and your parents are exactly what you needed for your life lessons.

29. Spread joy and happiness.

Be the example of what you want to see in the world. Focus on joy and happiness. Refuse to be cynical. Be the uplifting light in everyone's day. Believe in the possibility of miracles. Allow others to be happy.

30. Talk to yourself.
Be kind. Be loving. Talk often and with enthusiasm. Ask yourself hard questions. Challenge yourself to grow. Tell jokes to yourself. Read out loud to yourself.

31. Stand near the ocean whenever you have the chance.
The ocean air is charged with negative ions that attach themselves to free radicals. Think of it as Velcro for your negative energy. It is a fantastic way to clean up any negativity.

32. Eat real food.
Eat fruit. Eat vegetables. Buy meat from a butcher who sings while he works. Buy full-fat peanut butter and sour cream. If you are going to drink soda pop, drink the real thing and avoid the artificial sweeteners. Don't bother with low-fat cookies. If you are going to indulge, eat the real thing.

33. Give money or food to the homeless.
They are people just like you and me. Whenever I see a homeless person I remember that they are someone's child. I treat them the way I'd want a stranger to treat my child in the same situation.

34. Baby-sit for a single parent.
Make an offer to give a single parent a break and baby-sit for free. Most single parents are struggling to make ends meet and also have very little time for themselves. You can also offer to

take their kids out so they can enjoy a little peace and quiet in their own home.

35. Think about world peace every single day.

Meditate about it. Pray about it. Visualize it. Believe it. World peace will only come about when the collective consciousness can envision it. Focus on peace. Be peaceful inside so that we can start to see it on the outside.

36. Bless your enemies and your challenges.

Remember that there are no mistakes and your greatest challenges represent your greatest growth opportunities. Therefore, your enemies and your challenges are the best things that could happen to you. Send only loving energy to your adversaries. Try to understand the lesson that is being presented.

37. Cheer for the opposing team.

What would it take for you to be happy when the other team scores a basket? Think about how good it feels when you get what you want. It feels the same when someone else gets what they want. Wish that feeling on other people.

38. Sing louder than anyone else.

Set an example for the people around you. If you sing loudly, others will follow suit. There is nothing more inspiring than an entire stadium singing at the top of its lungs.

39. Acknowledge someone at least once a day.

This is a form of gratitude and it makes the other person feel really good. People love to know when they have made a dif-

ference in your life. Tell them. It is especially important to acknowledge your children, your partner and your parents.

40. Say grace or be thankful before every meal.
Hold hands. Take a moment to be present to the gratitude you
feel for being fortunate to have food to eat. Bless the earth for
providing the food. Hold the vision that it is possible for everyone on Earth to get what they need.

41. Lead by example.
Be the first to do something. Use actions, not words. Be positive and encouraging. Allow others to follow in their own way.

42. Smile.
It's a gift you can give for free. It is a great way to exercise your
face. Look people in the eye when you smile at them. Smile
with your whole body. Smiling triggers a happy state in most
people. It's a fantastic way to shift quickly.

> *"We cannot hold a torch to light another's path*
> *without brightening our own."*
> *– Ben Sweetland*

COMPANION ONLINE RESOURCE	**THINK AGAIN!** Visit www.GinaML.com/Chapters to get a summarized version of this chapter for your quick reference.

FREE RESOURCES

You are constantly making the choice to THINK or SINK as you navigate the circumstances of your life. Author Gina Mollicone-Long has prepared these resources for you to give you some extra tools for those moments that you aren't actually reading your copy of *Think or Sink*. These resources will help keep you in the THINKing mindset regardless of what is going on around you.

Visit **www.GinaML.com/Resources**
to download these FREE resources:

THINK GOALS

Think Goal Setting

Most people know what they want but get overwhelmed by the details. Goal setting a process that can be easily mastered by starting with the big picture and working your way down. Download this free goal-setting template to help you break down ANY goal into manageable chunks.

Unconscious Thinking Power

We often refer to the conscious mind as the goal *setter* and the unconscious mind as the goal *getter*. Download this free report on the directives of the unconscious mind so that you can learn to maximize your own built-in powerful goal GETTING machine.

FOR THINKERS

THINK LIFE

Think Quickly

We can make a new choice to THINK differently in any situation. Some situations are easier than others. Download this free short video to remind you of 42 quick things you can do to shift your experience anywhere, anytime.

Think Simple

It's a simple process for getting the results that you want. The process for creating your desired outcome is the same for all areas of your life including money, health, relationships, business and personal growth. Download this free worksheet template for The Simple Process so that you can design the life you love.

> Visit **www.GinaML.com/Resources** to download your FREE resources.

NOTES